Starters for Thinking

ROBERT FISHER

Acknowledgements

I am most grateful to all the people who have helped my research into *Starters for Thinking*. My thanks go to all the teachers who have shared their ideas and experiences with me and to the children who have shared their thoughts with me. Particular thanks go to Kevin Hogston, Lizann O'Conor, Marcello Staricoff and Julie Winyard for the ways in which they have inspired and informed this book.

First published in 2006 by
Nash Pollock Publishing
32 Warwick Street
Oxford OX4 1SX

9 8 7 6 5 4 3 2 1

Orders to:
York Publishing Services
64 Hallfield Road
Layerthorpe
York YO31 7ZQ

A catalogue record of this book is available from the British Library.

ISBN-10: 1 898255 48 2

ISBN-13: 978 1 898255 48 2

Design, typesetting and production management by Black Dog Design

Printed in Great Britain by The Cromwell Press, Trowbridge

Contents

Introduction

'*We need to think better if we are to become better people.*' Paul, age 10

Starters for Thinking are designed to be enjoyable, open-ended challenges suitable for all pupils. They aim to stimulate the brain and prepare the mind for learning by focusing attention and activating the neurons. They provide ideal starting points for thinking and what the poet W.B. Yeats called 'the fascination with what's difficult'. They draw on children's experiences and mental resources rather than on specific bits of subject knowledge. They are suitable for children working individually, in pairs, in groups or as a whole class. They offer children and teachers the freedom to experiment with thinking and to engage in creativity of mind. They aim to offer enjoyment and entertainment for curious minds and a stimulus for creative activity.

This introduction to the starters shows how they can be used to stimulate thinking and creativity in the classroom. It is divided into three sections:

- Why starters?
- How to use starters?
- What kinds of thinking?

Included in this book are about 500 starters for thinking, divided into 30 sections. Each section presents a different strategy or structure for thinking, illustrated with a range of challenges for children, in a double-page spread.

Starters can be used at the start of the day or at other times – at the start of any lesson, at the end of the day, or for homework. They can also provide activities for a Thinking Club, alongside other books in the *Stories for Thinking* series.

Starters for Thinking aim to engage children's brains in challenging and creative mental activity and develop their thinking skills. But why starters?

Why starters?

'*I'm quite good at thinking, I just need someone to start me up.*' Josh, age 8

There are many reasons why a 'starter for thinking' can provide a good way to start a day, session or lesson in school. These reasons include:

- to focus attention
- to challenge the mind
- to motivate and enjoy.

Focus attention

One of the challenges of teaching is to focus children's attention on learning. This can be a particular problem first thing in the morning when their heads are full of other things, after the physical and emotional rough and tumble of playtimes, or after protracted periods of passive activity. At such times merely saying 'Sit down and pay attention' may not be enough. They need an activity that grabs and holds their attention.

Our attention system has evolved to recognise dramatic changes that signal danger, and to ignore steady states of gradual change and subtle differences. Human attention is focused by sudden surprises. Having a starter for thinking ready on the board can be effective in capturing children's attention right from the beginning of a lesson or day. As Chris, age 10, says: 'I like to begin the day with something to think about.'

There are many reasons why children may be inattentive. They live in a televisual world where they are bombarded with information, flashing images and noise. They are prey to their own frustration and to the anger of others. Their minds can become flooded with their personal concerns. Researchers claim that children are suffering from more mental problems and stresses than ever before. No wonder many lack concentration in the classroom and are impulsive in their behaviour. As Kelly, aged 8, put it: 'In the morning my mind is buzzing – but not with school!'

What a good starter for thinking does is to help train children to hold and sustain attention. It challenges children to focus attention on relevant memories, experience and knowledge, and also to shift attention to what others are thinking. A good starter lights up the mind.

Being able to direct attention helps children to fight off distraction. Directed attention is needed to help them to process information effectively and to sort the important from the unimportant among the vast quantities of stimuli they encounter daily. Starters help children sustain attention through open-ended challenges with a range of options which link to their personal concerns, or which engage them in ways of looking at the world that are their own. Opportunities to share their thinking and to attend to the thinking of others help to shift and re-engage attention, as does discussing with children their own ability to focus attention, think and learn. As Jenny, aged 10, said, 'It helps to talk about it afterwards.'

Memory is the daughter of attention. We cannot expect children to focus on or remember what they do unless we help to train their attention. Some specific attention-training strategies are included in this book (see Meditation, p.36, Visualisation, p.64). One strategy for focusing attention is to use chants. Choose a word to chant with the children, preferably something calming like 'Think', 'Clear' or 'Still'. Get the class to chant the word over and over again to clear and focus the mind. Other strategies for getting attention and helping children to practise directing and sustaining attention include using music (Music, p.38) or pictures (Picture This, p.50). As Cheryl, aged 10, said: 'The mind can be trained,' and we are never too young or too old for that training.

Challenge the mind

We need to develop in children habits of mind that will help them to cope with the unexpected, to make sense of the incomplete, and to cope with challenge, change and complexity. Their future lives will be full of unexpected challenges and opportunities, and they will need creative minds to cope and thrive in a continually changing world. We need to begin these challenges early. Brain research has shown that most of the growth in the human brain occurs in early childhood. By the age of six or seven, the brain in the majority of children is approximately 90% of its adult size. This implies that cognitive challenge is especially important in the early years of education, though of course it continues to be important at all stages.

Starters challenge the mind by confronting it with the unexpected. The first challenges in this book involve children thinking about themselves (About Me, p.14). Other challenges involve designs for a better world (p.22), a greener world (p.28), and a future world (p.32). Children are challenged to explore their feelings (p.26), to respond to philosophical questions (p.48) and to make informed choices (pp.24, 72). They have visual (pp.20, 50) and verbal (pp.18, 70) challenges. They are asked to process information (p.52), make decisions (p.66), solve problems (p.54) and explore imaginary worlds (p.64). In all more than 500 challenges are included, with ideas for many more ways to extend children's thinking, expand their consciousness and build intelligence.

More detail is given below on the specific thinking skills and habits of mind developed by these starters. One reason why a mental challenge can be so fruitful is that when children succeed it motivates and raises self esteem. As Polly, aged 10, put it: 'When your brain is working well it makes you feel good.'

Motivate and enjoy

Starters aim to motivate and engage children. One reason why starters motivate is that children do not see them as 'work'. Starters provide opportunities for creativity and self-expression without pre-determined outcomes and without having to be marked by others. A good starter does not have one 'right answer' but many possible answers. A starter is like a challenging kind of play, where children are free to experiment, hypothesise, and juggle with ideas. They invite children to draw upon their own experiences, knowledge and ideas. The open-ended nature of starters mean they have something to offer children of all abilities. They are ideal for independent work or for homework. Nick, aged 10, says: 'I like to do thinking in my own way.' Keri responds: 'It's also fun to take out your thinking and share it with others.'

Enjoyment is motivating. Sessions, therefore, should be kept relaxed and playful. The creative juices flow best when children are relaxed and enjoying themselves and feel free to take risks and be playful. They might invite children into an enjoyable world of make believe that all could enter. Start by asking 'What if ... ?' (p.68) and 'If ... then?' For example:

- If you were someone else who would you be? Talk of your past life.

- If you had a magic carpet where would you wish to go? Why?
- If you could repeat a favourite moment of your life, what would it be?

The varied nature of the starters in this book means that they will often, though not always, connect with the interests of children. Sometimes children will become so motivated that they will want to continue researching a starter in their own time or to create their own starters. When asked which of the starters he liked best, Danny, age 10, said: 'I like the starters that take you in your mind where you have not been before. They're the best.'

How to use starters

'*There are many ways of being a good teacher.*' Tom, age 10

There are many approaches to using the starters. Be creative with them by using, adapting or developing any of the ideas and adding your own. This book contains 30 themes which provide frameworks for thinking. Each theme has an introduction to the skills and strategies being developed, with links to thinking processes involved and other themes, followed by a list of suggested starters.

Some teachers use the starters in a programmed way, for example at the start of each day. Others use them in a serendipitous way, whenever a time in the day seems suitable. Some like to plan a series of daily starters around a particular theme; others prefer the variety of choosing a different type of starter each day. They can also be used as starters for staff meetings or inset sessions. As one teacher put it: 'Sharing a teaching idea is a good warm-up for a staff meeting. After all thinking teachers is what it's all about – or should be.'

The whole cycle of a starter will usually take about 15–20 minutes. A session will usually follow this pattern:

- teacher presents a starter for thinking
- children respond and record
- the thinking is shared

Presenting a starter

The children are all lined up outside a classroom door at the start of day. 'What are you waiting for?' I ask. 'We are waiting for our teacher to open the door.' 'Why?' 'Because we don't know what he's put on the board. There's something different every day.' 'What is it?' I ask. 'It's something for us to think about!' The girl's eyes shine. The door of the classroom opens ...

Many teachers write a starter on the board before the children come into class, so that when they enter they know they are entering a thinking and learning environment to do a task. Some teachers have music playing. There has been much research into the 'Mozart effect', the effect of music on children's thinking and problem solving abilities. The evidence is mixed, but many projects have reported improvements in children's responses to cognitive tasks when music of some complexity such as light classical or folk music is playing. It is not clear whether this has to do with music stimulating brain activity, or its relaxing and enhancing effects on the mood of listeners – or both. The same music does not affect all listeners in the same way. Some children like music to accompany their thinking, others do not. The same is true of adults.

A starter for thinking is more than just listening to music or doing some repeated aerobic exercises, useful as these may be in focusing attention. A starter aims to exercise the mind by getting children to think, by challenging their minds. It stretches not their physical bodies but their mental resources. A common way to start children thinking is to set a question that directly derives from the outcome of the last lesson (which may have come through wishing to assess something specific which they have been taught, or to apply what they know to a new area). Children could be asked to make up their own quiz questions to ask the rest of class, based on the week's work/topic. Or the starter might prepare them for their next research topic, for example through doing a KWL grid. As one teacher suggests: 'Choose a topic e.g. rainforests. Students draw three columns headed K/W/L: K = Know (what they know), W = Want to know, and L= Learnt. Choose a topic. Ask children to write at least three things in each of the first two columns, then share, discuss and add more to your grid.'

Another way is through a Question of the Week. As one teacher describes it: 'At the beginning of the week a question is placed somewhere in the room (I choose by the door) either linked to the curriculum or not, but it must require the children to go away and think about or research their answer. They give me the answer, at a convenient time, and by Friday we discuss the answer. I do encourage the children to take part by offering team points! Interesting to see the enthusiasm – those who always have an answer do show a keen interest in learning – and it is clearly seen even with the children who do not offer an answer.'

Another teacher likes to use problems as starters for thinking. Thinking about an imaginary problem loosens children's thinking and 'gets the creative juices flowing'. She gives an example: 'Imagine you are going to a deserted island. You can take ten people with you but you cannot take family or friends! Who would you take and why? Children can then be encouraged to discuss their individual choices in smaller or table groups. Children could be asked to agree a final list of just three from their collaborative choices. This gives raise to interesting debate and discussion as children put forward cases for their choices.'

One teacher puts up on the board some new phrases in the foreign language the class are learning, or children could be asked to think of and practise vocabulary in that language. For example, show a picture of a person on the whiteboard. Ask pupils to start thinking by inventing a life story for this person in a foreign language. Other ideas include inventing a dream house, or designing their own menu in a foreign language.

Another teacher challenges his children to speedwrite. He suggests: 'Write one word on the board, such as 'Blue'. Children then write whatever comes into their heads about the word for a set time, for example two minutes. They share their writing with a partner. They choose together their most interesting words or ideas to share with the rest of the class. These are recorded on the board.'

Starters are not just about words. They could be about visual, mathematical or musical challenges. Some teachers use Odd One Out (p.46) as starters in numeracy lessons, for example by asking which of three numbers is the odd one out, for example 9, 17 and 36 (or what reasons might there be for each of these numbers to be the odd one out?). Objects work just as well as starters for thinking. Give each child a random object from a special box, e.g. a piece of material, foil or paper. What could it be? What does it make them think of? What story?

Responding and recording

Children need not only a stimulus to start thinking, but also the space to 'see what they think' and to record their thinking. One way to provide a thinking space is through a personal notebook where children can record their thoughts. This book can go under a number of names including 'learning log', 'jotter', or 'think book' (Fisher, 2004). If it is a *personal* notebook it means that a child may or may not show it to teachers or others, for it is about recording one's personal thinking. Such a 'thinking' book provides the opportunity for a child to express and make explicit to themself (or to others) their thinking in words or pictures.

Having a personal book in which to record what one thinks and learns is common to a range of people. It is a common practice of artists, writers, researchers, scientists and engineers to keep a written record of what they observe, think and do. Such books are used to jot down what the writer, artist or researcher thought or did, their reactions, the questions that occur to them and their tentative conclusions. This can be done in quick notes, sketches, mindmaps or in any personal kind of writing. A think book or learning log invites children to become real researchers.

A 'think book' provides children with a private space to:

- think, question and experiment with ideas
- record their thinking and learning in their own way
- reflect on, evaluate and make sense of experience.

Think books enable learners to improve their own thinking through reflection. This builds intelligence at cognitive, emotional and metacognitive levels. At a cognitive level it enables children to exercise the thinking skills and processes that are discussed below. At an emotional level it enables them to explore their feelings and to express personal preferences. At a metacognitive level it enables pupils to develop the ability to plan, monitor, evaluate and reflect on their own thinking and learning.

We often have learning experiences without really thinking about them. Children can respond to the starters for thinking in their think books. These also provide the opportunity for short, ungraded and unedited pieces of personal writing as a way to promote genuine reflection on any learning activity. Some teachers ask students to make entries in their logs during the last five minutes of class or after each completed week of class. Again the message here is that short, frequent bursts of writing are more productive over time than infrequent, longer sessions.

Here are some ways of using think books to start and record thinking:

Summarise learning objectives	before an activity, ask children to summarise the learning objectives in their own words
Pause to write	after a learning activity or discussion, pause and ask children to think/write about their learning
Pause to paraphrase	ask children to clarify an idea by writing a paraphrase in their own words
Respond to key ideas	during a lesson, have thinking time (a mini-plenary) to reflect on key ideas of the lesson
Reflect on learning	following a lesson, discussion, or activity, ask children to reflect on key ideas or success criteria
Ask questions	ask children to write questions about what they want to know about a topic
Write memos	invite children to record what they need to remember

There is no one best way of stimulating students to write in their journals. Questions or 'starters' can stimulate thinking and help frame their reflections. Some teachers display a few key questions permanently in their classrooms. They do this because they want their children to internalise the sorts of questions that good learners ask themselves. Such questions might include:

- What have you learnt?
- What did you find interesting?
- What did you find hard?
- What do you need to remember?

Some statement 'starters' to stimulate a thinking response include:

The questions I want to ask are …

I wonder … How … ? Why … ?

I think/feel/believe …

My problem is …

My solution is …

The key ideas (learning objectives) are …

I now think …

I need to remember …

During the school day children might for example be asked to write non-stop for five minutes on any specific topic they are studying. The purpose is for students to find out what they know about the topic, explore new ideas, and find out what they need to learn. In maths children can be asked to write an explanation to another student of how to do a maths problem. In history children could place themselves in a historical period or event and write about it from the point of view of someone who was there, focusing on the what, where, why, how, when, and what if. Or children can write a dialogue between themselves and a person from a different time or place. As Gail, aged 9, said: 'In most books you have to write what the teacher says but in a think book your mind can wander.'

Sharing thinking

Starters also provide the chance for children to share their thinking with others, in paired work, in small groups or for sharing with the whole class. They help create a community of learners, an ethos and a culture of learning. As Tracey, aged 7, said: 'I like seeing the thinking of other people. It gives me something to think.'

An open-ended question, like those in this book, can result in responses that stimulate further thinking. In response to the question: 'How do you get a bigger brain?' Sarah, aged 8, said: 'You get a bigger brain by adding to it what others have thought that you would not have thought.' As Sarah implies, it is good to think for yourself but it is better if you can share your thinking with others. In that way you get more ideas, expand your consciousness and make new and unexpected connections in your mind.

There are many ways to share thinking. A common and effective strategy is 'think-pair-share', where children are given thinking time for personal response, then time to share their thinking with a partner, then opportunities to share this with the class or group. The children's thinking can be extended by asking them to create their own variations of a given puzzle or problem. Many of the starters in this book include further suggestions (given in brackets) or invite children to develop their own ideas.

Starters can be built into the teaching methods you already use. Some teachers use circle time strategies to encourage the sharing of thinking. According to one teacher, Counting Circle is good for forging relationships with a class, particularly a new class. He summarises the strategy as: 'The aims of this activity are setting goals, listening and concentrating, and cooperation. Sit in a circle. All close eyes. The teacher says '1'. Any child says '2', another says '3' and so on. If more than one say a number at same time, the count goes back to one. The aim is to get to a higher number each time.'

Other teachers have a Learning Board as a starter for thinking at the end of the day, where children jot down what they think they learned that day. On the learning board some teachers also put a starter for thinking for children to take away with them at the end of the day to think about and share next morning. Whatever the strategy, the aim is to help children 'get their thinking out and share it with others'. But what kinds of thinking?

What kinds of thinking?

'*We need to think better if we are going to be better people.*' Paul, age 10

Starters for Thinking aims to develop thinking, but what kinds of thinking? The thinking processes involved in a starter or any other kind of learning activity can be divided into three kinds of mental processing:

- thinking skills and processes: thinking and cognition
- emotional response: thinking and feeling
- me-cognition: thinking and metacognition

In recent years there has been growing interest across the world in ways of developing children's thinking and learning skills. This interest has been fed by new knowledge about how the brain works and how people learn, and by evidence that specific interventions can improve children's thinking and intelligence. The particular ways in which people apply their minds to solving problems are called *thinking skills*. Many researchers suggest that thinking skills are essential to effective learning, though not all agree on the definition of this term. If thinking is how children make sense of learning then developing their thinking skills will help them get more out of learning and life. But what are thinking skills?

Thinking skills and processes

Thinking skills are not mysterious entities existing somewhere in the mind. Nor are they like mental muscles that have a physical presence in the brain. What the term refers to is the human capacity to think in conscious ways to achieve certain purposes. Such processes include remembering, questioning, forming concepts, planning, reasoning, imagining, solving problems, making decisions and judgements, translating thoughts into words and so on. Thinking skills are ways in which humans exercise the *sapiens* part of being *homo sapiens*.

A skill is commonly defined as a practical ability in doing something or succeeding in a task. Usually we refer to skills in particular contexts, such as being 'good at cooking' but they can also refer to general areas of performance, such as having a logical mind, a good memory, being creative and so on. A thinking skill is a practical ability to think in ways that are judged to be more or less effective or skilled. They are the habits of intelligent behaviour learned through practice: for example, children can become better at giving reasons or asking questions the more they practise doing so.

If thinking skills are the mental capacities we use to investigate the world, solve problems and make judgements, then to identify every such skill would be to enumerate all the capacities of the human mind. Such a list would be endless. The starters in this book stimulate a range of thinking skills and processes. Relevant thinking skills are listed at the foot of each theme page. These skills and processes could be discussed with children when they have shared their thinking at the end of each starter.

All thinking requires cognition, firstly through perception - the capacity to perceive sensory stimulus. Cognition enables the mind to process and transform information and to reflect on it as well as on our own thinking. Good thinking is developed through a range of challenges that exercise the 'thinking muscles' of the mind. Such thinking involves many processes and requires effort. As a child said about one of the starters: 'Thinking about this is more tiring than running round!'

The following are some of the thinking skills and thinking processes exercised and developed by the starters in this book:

Thinking skills	***Thinking processes***
Cognition	– focused attention, concentration, memorising, visualising
Information processing	– classifying/categorising, comparing/contrasting, ordering
Enquiry	– asking questions, predicting, problem posing, researching
Reasoning	– analysing, logical thinking, reasoning
Creative thinking	– generating ideas, imagining, hypothesising, metaphorical/analogical thinking
Evaluation	– assessing, checking, decision making, judging by criteria
Metacognition	– me-cognition, self awareness, thinking about thinking

Research by Piaget and Vygotsky suggested that thinking skills and processes are developed by *cognitive challenge* (Fisher 2005). As we said earlier, we now know that most of the growth in the human brain occurs in early childhood. Cognitive challenge is important at all stages, but especially in the early years of education. Young children need to share their thinking more through talking and drawing than writing, but they have as much need for starters for thinking as older children. Good teachers get children thinking at whatever age. Or as Tom, aged 10, put it: 'A good teacher makes you think ... even when you don't want to.'

Emotional response

Psychologists and philosophers have helped to extend our understanding of the term 'thinking', including the importance of dispositions, such as attention and motivation, commonly associated with thinking. This has prompted a move away from a simple model of 'thinking skills' as isolated cognitive capacities to a view of thinking as inextricably connected to emotions and dispositions, including 'emotional intelligence', which is our ability to understand our own emotions and the emotions of others (Goleman 1995).

There has been much research into how what we say and think affects our emotions. Thinking, saying or writing positive things can lift our spirits. One of the purposes of *Starters for Thinking* is enjoyment: when they work well they help you to be happy in and with your thinking. Seligman (2002), in his research into human happiness' offers five starters for us and our children to 'think happy' (see below).

Think happy

- Think and write of five things that make you happy and say why.
- Write three things that you can do well and say why.
- Write three things that you have learnt this week and say how you learnt each one.
- Write what you are proudest to have achieved and say why.
- Write a note to thank someone who has really helped you. Say how they helped you.

Adapted from: Seligman (2002), *Authentic Happiness*

What a good teacher does is to help create the positive emotional conditions for learning to take place. They also make children think about the conditions that create happiness in learning and in life. The following is a recipe for a happy class by David, aged 11:

My recipe for a happy class

INGREDIENTS

1 pinch of sharing

1/2 a cup of confidence

1 tbsp of enjoyment

6 tsp of cheerfulness

5 oz of communication

1/2 kg of good looks

1 lb of cheerfulness

250g of co-operation

10g of behaviour

1 kg of discipline

1 really nice teacher (grated)

500 ml of kindness

METHOD

Mix the confidence, communication and co-operation together in a large bowl. Add the enjoyment, the cheerfulness and the good looks to the mixture. Beat together the behaviour, the discipline and add to the mixture. Bake the cake at 200° C in a round tin 15cm deep and 45 cm in diameter for 1 week. Once the cake is baked, take it out of the oven and sprinkle the teacher on top.

The cake makes 10 helpings.

(from Fisher R. (2005), *Teaching Children to Learn*, p.152)

Me-cognition

There is a growing realisation that we need not only to teach cognitive skills and strategies but also to develop the higher cognitive functions involved in metacognition. Metacognition involves thinking about one's own thinking. Developing metacognition involves making learners aware of themselves as thinkers and learners, developing knowledge of oneself, or what I call 'me-cognition'.

'Me-cognition' is about what I know, think and feel about myself. It involves applying our thinking skills and emotional awareness to self-understanding, for example by finding answers to questions such as:

What do I think about myself?

What do I know about myself?

What do I feel about myself?

What makes me different from other people?

Am I a good learner?

What would help me become a good learner?

Me-cognition involves being aware of what one knows, what one has learnt, what one can and cannot do and ways to improve one's learning or achievement.

A good curriculum is not simply a collection of separate items of subject knowledge but is underpinned by the skills of lifelong learning. Good teaching is partly about achieving particular curriculum objectives but is also about developing general thinking skills and learning behaviours. A growing number of programmes and strategies aim to help teachers develop children's thinking and learning across the curriculum (Fisher 2005). Teachers are developing 'teaching for thinking' approaches in new directions, integrating them into everyday teaching to create 'thinking classrooms', and developing whole school policies to create 'thinking schools'.

This book offers one approach to creating a thinking classroom (for more see Staricoff & Rees 2005). Much scope remains for your own research into new teaching strategies that will develop children's thinking and learning. Record, share and review your own ideas, strategies and starters for thinking. Share your starters with us to improve future editions of this book.

Recent test results show that standards in schools are rising – but slowly. Could the teaching of thinking provide a key to raising achievement? The experience of many teachers suggests that when pupils are taught the habits of effective thinking they grow in confidence, their learning is enriched and they are better prepared to face the challenges of the future. Children think so too – as Arran, aged 9, put it: 'When you get out in the real world you have to think for yourself, that's why we need to practise it in school.' So let's, as teachers and parents, be their starters for thinking.

References

Fisher R., *Stories for Thinking* (1996), *Games for Thinking* (1997), *Poems for Thinking* (1997), *First Stories for Thinking* (1999), *First Poems for Thinking* (2000), *Values for Thinking* (2001), Oxford: Nash Pollock Publishing

Fisher R. (2003), *Teaching Thinking: Philosophical Enquiry in the Classroom*, London: Continuum

Fisher R., (2004), 'Think Books', *Teaching Thinking*, Spring 2004, pp.18-23

Fisher R. (2nd ed, 2005), *Teaching Children to Think*, Cheltenham: Stanley Thornes

Fisher R. (2nd ed, 2005), *Teaching Children to Learn*, Cheltenham: Stanley Thornes

Goleman D. (1996), *Emotional Intelligence*, London: Bloomsbury

Seligman P. (2002), *Authentic Happiness*, London: Simon & Schuster (www.authentichappiness.com)

Staricoff M. & Rees M. (2005), *Start Thinking*, Birmingham: Questions Publishing

1 About Me

'There are things in my mind that nobody knows. Sometimes I don't even know them myself.' James, age 10

We all know some things that no one else knows, including what we are at any moment thinking or feeling. Because we are thinking and feeling beings and our thoughts and feelings change over time, '*What am I thinking?*' and *What am I feeling?*' are always questions we can ask of ourselves or of others. Humans have access to unique and special knowledge of themselves in the private theatre of their thoughts. 'Thinking about me', or me-cognition, is a fundamental capacity of human thinking – and a good starter for thinking.

'Me-cognition' is about what I know and think about myself. It involves finding answers to questions such as: *What do I think about myself? What do I know about myself? What do I feel about myself? What makes me different from other people? What makes me special? What makes 'me' me?*

Such questions have challenged philosophers, psychologists and scientists down the centuries. Outside the oracle at Delphi was the injunction 'Know thyself'. For the ancient Greeks this was the hardest challenge to thinking and the highest form of wisdom.

'Me-cognition' is a capacity for self-understanding that all humans possess. It is a form of personal intelligence (what psychologist Howard Gardner calls 'intra-personal intelligence'). It is expressed in a child's ability to be aware of what they think and feel and of their personal preferences. It involves processes of metacognition, that is, thinking about one's own thinking.

The skills of me-cognition are developed when the individual learner is given a voice and a choice in what they think about themselves and their lives. Such self-reflection lies at the heart of personalised learning. As Joel, age 9, put it: 'A good teacher makes what you think matters.'

Asking children about their personal lives, hopes and fears makes good starters for thinking, because it focuses on what they think, know and have experienced. Many kinds of questions can encourage children to think about themselves and their lives. As Tom, age 10, said: 'You don't really know what you think until someone asks.' The following questions may produce some interesting and unexpected answers.

Thinking processes: Me-cognition, metacognition, self awareness

Links: Analogies, p.18; Feelings, p.26; Make a List, p.34; Meditation, p.36. See also: 'Thinking about me' in *First Poems for Thinking*, pp.32-3; 'Thinking about me' in *Poems for Thinking*, pp.54-5; 'Who am I?' in *Stories for Thinking*, p.114

Starters for thinking

- Describe yourself to someone who has never met you.
- If you could be anyone else in the world, who would you be and why?
- What would be your perfect day? Begin from waking up in the morning.
- What things are you most afraid of? Say why.
- If you could change five things about yourself, what would you change?
- Who are your heroes and heroines? Say why.
- What dreams have you had (nicest, nastiest, funniest or strangest dream)? What dream would you like to have?
- If you were giving a party, who would you invite and why?
- You have been granted three wishes. What would you wish for and why?
- Write five things that you can do well. Say why.
- If you couldn't hear anything, what five things would you miss most and why?
- What would be your ideal holiday or day trip? Who would you go with? Why?
- Think of five things you like to smell. Say why you like them.
- What makes you smile?
- What would you miss most if you could not see? How would your life change?
- If you could be famous, what would you like to be famous for? Why?
- What are your earliest memories? Describe as much as you can remember.
- What do you want to be when you grow up? Why? What do you need to do?
- What is you favourite time of day? Give five or more reasons for your choice. (Favourite day of the week, month, season of the year).
- 'I wish I could ...' What five things would you like to be able to do and why?
- Write what you are proudest to have achieved. Say why.

2 Alphabeticals

'I know what everyone's favourite letter is ... I.' James, age 11

Words are the tools for thinking. In western languages words are structured out of the letters of the alphabet. One way that we structure thinking is by finding a pattern and putting things in order, for example by putting things in a numerical order. Another way is alphabetically, by putting things in alphabetical order. The following starters use knowledge of the alphabet to order and structure thinking. Within the alphabetical structure there is opportunity to exercise memory and to be creative in experimenting with words and making alternative word choices.

An A-Z can be created out of any body of knowledge, for example the topic you are studying. It is a popular starter for thinking with children, particularly if they work in pairs. It can lead on to an interest in the alphabet and into ways that letters have been used and developed in different times and places.

The alphabet is arguably the most important human invention. The earliest known alphabet was the 'North Semitic' developed in about 1700 BC in Palestine, consisting of 22 consonant letters. The Arabic, Hebrew and Phoenician alphabets were based on this one, as was the Greek, which added four letters for vowels. The Greek alphabet became the model for the ancient Roman and later our alphabet (Modern Roman). The word 'alphabet' comes from the Greek alpha, meaning 'a', and beta, meaning 'b'. There are dozens of alphabets of different sizes. The smallest from the Solomon Islands has 11 letters, while the largest from Khmer uses 74. With the alphabet, history and human thinking could be recorded rather then memorised and so preserved forever and for all people.

An interesting investigation for children to is to find out the most frequently used letters by tallying the times they appear in a text such as a reading book or newspaper, and then charting the results. The following are other ways of using the alphabet as starters for thinking.

Thinking processes: classifying, creative thinking, ordering

Links: Make a List, p.34; Word Play, p.70

Starters for thinking

- Create an A-Z of things related to school.
- Create an alphabet of crazy characters, using the same initial letter to describe them: e.g. 'Agatha is an artist living in an attic.'
- Write an A-Z of healthy foods.
- Try to create an A-Z of the names of towns and cities.
- Make up a sentence which includes every letter of the alphabet.
- Create an alphabet of adjectives to describe animals, e.g. 'angry ant', 'blue baboon', 'crafty cat' etc.
- Write an A-Z of girls' names (or boys' names).
- Think of as many words as you can where the letters of the word are in alphabetical order, e.g. 'act'
- Create an alphabet of sports and games.
- Make up a sentence where each word begins with the next letter of the alphabet (first word starts with a-, second with b- and so on). See how far you can get.
- Make an A-Z of things you would find in your bedroom.
- Sort the capital letters of the alphabet into different groups, putting those with similar shapes together.
- Make an A-Z of jobs that people do.
- Predict which letters of the alphabet we use most often. Choose a passage from a reading book and count (tally) how many times each letter is used. What do you discover?
- Write an A-Z of anything that is on or by the roadside.
- Can you write the alphabet backwards? Can you say it without looking at the letters?
- Pack an alphabetical suitcase, an A-Z of items for a holiday.

3 Analogies

'I am like a grape, just one of a bunch, but I am full of juicy goodness.'
Michelle, age 10

The ability of the mind to make connections is the basis of analogical thinking. It is a skill that all human minds possess, but which needs developing. One way to develop this skill is the technique of creating comparison conceits.

A 'conceit' is a comparison of dissimilar things and was used by metaphysical poets such as John Donne. The technique forms the basis of synectics, a cognitive strategy which mobilises both sides of the brain (through the comparison of the dissimilar). 'Comparison conceits' can stimulate creative thinking and problem solving.

An important strategy in creative thinking and problem solving is being able to see an issue or problem in different ways, making the familiar strange so that we see new connections and possibilities. The following are three methods of creating metaphor for helping to see the familiar in new ways:

- Personal analogy – imagining being a thing, for example: *How are you like a candle?*
- Direct analogy – making a simple comparison, for example: *How is a teacher like a tuna sandwich?*
- Symbolic analogy – creating a compressed conflict (oxymoron), for example: *What is an example of a careful collision?*

Carl Sandburg, the American poet, once said: 'Poetry is the synthesis of hyacinths and biscuits.' Here he was taking two unrelated words or images and putting them together to make the familiar strange. One way of doing this is to take two unrelated words or ideas and try to join them with a linking thought. If what we think about one thing is also true of another we are reasoning by analogy. For example when children were asked, 'How is summer like a bridge?', one child answered, 'Because they are both full of comings and goings.' When asked for reasons why a teacher was like a ham sandwich, one response was, 'Because they both have a sell-by date!'

Children can also be encouraged to create their own comparison conceits (analogies) by choosing two different things at random and asking questions such as:

In what ways might these things be similar?

What do you know about one object that might be true of the other?

How might they be compared?

Children can write or draw their responses to the following challenges in analogical thinking.

Thinking processes: analogical thinking, creative thinking, metaphorical thinking

Links: About Me, p.14

Starters for thinking

Personal analogies

- If you were green what would you be? Why?
- In what ways are you like a bunch of grapes?
- In what ways are you like gold?
- In what ways are you like a cloud?
- What kind of furniture are you? (or food, drink, toy etc.)
- What kind of animal are you?
- How is your life like a river?

Direct analogies

- How is a teacher like a ham sandwich?
- Why is summer like a bridge?
- How is the sea like a mirror?
- How is a cup like the world?
- Which animal is like a rubber band?
- Which colour is quickest?
- How is a boat like a banana?
- How is a ... like a ... ? (Choose objects or events that seem quite unrelated, or ask children to choose.)

4 Creative Shapes

'*It's easy to see a shape but it's hard to move it in your mind.*' Ben, age 8

One simple way to be creative with shapes is for the teacher to draw a simple shape, symbol or diagram and ask: 'What could it be?' 'How many different things could it be?' 'What is the most interesting thing it could be?' This calls for creative thinking but also challenges their spatial intelligence.

Spatial intelligence is the ability to represent the visual-spatial world internally in the mind, to perceive it accurately, and to use these perceptions to solve problems or be creative. It involves sensitivity to line, shape, form and space, and to the way these are related. It includes the capacity to visualize, to graphically represent visual or spatial ideas, and to orient oneself appropriately in a spatial context. It is a form of non-verbal reasoning that enables us to see visual patterns and to generate, retain, and transform visual shapes. Spatial abilities are important for higher-order thinking in science, technology and maths. Successful sailors, engineers, packers, surgeons and taxi-drivers have a highly developed spatial intelligence.

A person with spatial intelligence has the ability to form a mental model of a spatial world. This spatial awareness gives them skills in drawing, puzzle-solving, mazes, and tasks requiring fine-motor manipulation. The ability to see a whole in an incomplete form (a 'gestalt'), as well as the ability to identify specific shapes within a complex pattern, are also functions of spatial intelligence. Spatial thinking enables people to process visual information like pictures, maps, and plans. Without the ability to comprehend and interpret visual information, something as apparently straightforward as remembering how to get to the front door of our house (from the living room) would be beyond us. This ability is, therefore, a vital aspect of human thinking.

There is an interesting link between spatial thinking and music. Research in the USA has shown that music lessons, and even simply listening to music (for example a Mozart sonata), can enhance children's abilities to perform spatial tasks like making paper sculpture.

Spatial intelligence can be developed through spatial tasks and problems which help children to:

- perceive shapes and visual patterns accurately
- recreate or alter the images of shapes and patterns on paper
- recreate or alter the images of shapes and patterns in the mind.

Such tasks can be challenging, as spatial transformations in the mind place heavy demands on working memory.

Thinking processes: Creative thinking, spatial thinking, visual thinking

Links: Picture This, p.50; Visualisation, p.64

Starters for thinking

- Use six lines to draw a shape made of triangles. How many triangles can you make? (Try with other numbers of lines.)
- Copy this 2D shape. How many 3D shapes could this 2D shape be part of? (*Draw a 2D shape, e.g. a circle.*)
- How many different ways are there to arrange five squares? One side of each square must be next to another square. (How many ways are there to arrange three cubes?)
- Can you draw a mirror image of this shape? (*Draw a shape or shapes.*)
- Draw a map of your route to school, adding as much detail as you can.
- What shapes can you see in this diagram? Draw your own shape puzzle. (*Draw a shape puzzle, e.g. a tangram – see appendix, p.75 for examples.*)
- Can you get through this maze? Draw your own maze. (*Show an example of a maze – see appendix, p.74 for examples.*)
- Write your name in mirror writing. (*Write a message in mirror writing.*)
- How many things can you draw that look (circular, square, triangular, diamond-shaped, rectangular, etc.)? Label each drawing.
- Draw an upside down picture of this. (*Show a geometric pattern or other image.*)
- Draw a pyramid from as many viewpoints as you can.
- Listen to these instructions for drawing a picture. (*Dictate instructions for drawing a geometric picture, for children to draw listening to your instructions.*) Now draw your own geometric pictures, without showing your partner. Take turns to describe your pictures for your partners to draw.

5 Designing a Better World

'*I wish we could make a better world.*' Sophie, age 8

The man-made world is as it is but it does not have to stay that way. We can help our children design a better world by helping them design an improvement to something in this world or design something new.

One teacher encourages her six year-olds to think of themselves as designers of the future by giving each of them an 'Inventions' book. This is a book of large plain pages in which the children are encouraged to draw their own inventions. Sometimes the teacher will give them a starter (design brief) like 'Invent a dog-exercising machine'; at other times, at home or in spare time at school, the children are free to draw and experiment with their ideas. Their teacher comments: 'What is important is not so much what they design but the confidence they get from being designers and inventors.'

Drawing is a wonderful way of making thinking visible. A child may not find it easy to express thinking in words, but can always attempt to express it visually, and may find it easier to understand something in visual terms. We are primarily visual animals: over half the brain's capacity is taken up with processing visual stimuli. Children's ability to generate ideas through drawing far exceeds their ability to turn their ideas into reality. When posed with intriguing design problems such as a dog-exercising machine, a machine to weigh an elephant, a sleep machine, an improvement to the human body, or a way to stop a cat and dog fighting, children of all ages can respond with lively and inventive drawings.

Speculative design is a valuable preparation for practical designing where the creative idea is actually constructed in suitable materials. It is in practical design that children learn the need to compromise between an ideal solution on paper and what can actually be achieved within the constraints of time, money, materials, facilities and technical ability.

Thinking processes: Creative thinking, evaluating, visual thinking

Links: Green Thinking, p.28; Into the Future, p.32; Problem Solving, p.54

Starters for thinking

- Design something that would help in the house.
- Design a new stamp to mark a special occasion.
- Use the letters of your name to create a design for something.
- Invent a machine that would help you get up in the morning.
- Design a costume to wear at a fancy dress party.
- Design a poster to advertise your favourite book.
- Invent a new toy for a baby or young child.
- Imagine you have discovered a new plant. Draw what it looks like. Describe it.
- Design a machine that could travel in time. What 'times' would you visit? Why?
- Design a pair of shoes. Explain how they are made and any special features.
- Design a wrapper for a new health food.
- Design a secret den or hideout.
- Re-design the human body – how would you improve it?
- Design a home for a pet animal.
- Design something to help protect your home or possessions from burglars.
- Design an improvement for a desk ... (or a door, chair, window etc.)
- Design an interesting hat. Could you make it? How?
- Design your ideal ... (house, bedroom, car, etc.)
- Design a book mark which would encourage young children to read.
- Use the pattern of a cobweb in the design of a new or unusual product.

6 Dilemmas

'*We have to puzzle what to believe.*' Kiran, age 8

We all face dilemmas in life. A dilemma is when we have a difficult choice between alternatives. What dilemmas do you face? What dilemmas do your children face? Dilemmas can provide good starters for thinking.

Dilemmas can come from many sources – stories, news items from papers or on TV, or from daily life. Dilemmas face us with many of our most important decisions in life. Invite the children to share dilemmas they have read, heard about or faced in their own lives, for example by having a 'problems box' or 'help box' where children can report anonymously any problems or dilemmas that concern them. Other dilemmas can come from open questions of a general nature, for example: *What do you do if you are being bullied?*

Real life is a complex affair and only rarely are the choices clear-cut. Here is a dilemma which faced a child on his way to school. He found a five pound note in the street. He picked it up. No one had seen him. What could he do? What should he do? The essence of creative thinking about problems is conditional thinking – considering all the alternatives, factors and possible choices in a situation. In the discussion about finding a £5 note the class was asked to discuss: *What choices does the finder have? Which is the right choice? Which choice would you make – what would you actually do? Why? What general rule applies here?*

The aim is to encourage flexibility of ideas, and to consider the creation of real choices. Follow-up questions might include:

- If you have a choice to make, who can help you decide?
- Have you ever faced a dilemma (difficult choice) in your life?
- If so, how did you decide what to do?

We all need resilience to face up to dilemmas in life and to defend what we believe is right. This is developed through practice. The following dilemmas provide starters for thinking and discussion.

Thinking processes: Decision-making, evaluating, reasoning

Links: Problem Solving, p.54; Philosophical Questions, p.48; Would You Rather ... ?, p.72

Starters for thinking

- What is a dilemma? Give an example.
- What dilemmas have you faced in your life?
- What dilemmas do other people face?

Discuss and compare different approaches to the following dilemmas.

What could you do? What should you do? What would you do? If ...

- You find a £10 note on the street.
- You see your best friend steal a packet of sweets from a shop.
- You have lent your friend your best pen and they have not returned it.
- You told your friend a secret and they told everyone else.
- You are being left out of games in the playground.
- You are being accused of something you have not done.
- A friend lends you a toy, and you lose it. Should you buy them a new one? What should you do?
- You are stranded on a desert island. (What ten things would want to have with you? List them in order of importance.)
- Two of your friends have an argument and refuse to speak to each other. How could you help them to sort out the problem?
- You are stranded on a desert island. You can take three people with you, but not family or friends! Who would you take and why? (Who else would you like to take and why?)
- You have promised your mother not to eat crisps on the way home from school, but you do. Your mother finds a crisp packet in your pocket, and asks where it comes from. What would you say?
- You must decide ... (e.g. Should children be allowed to wear what they like to school?) What are the arguments for and against?

7 Feelings

'*I don't know what I feel until I think about it.*' Karen, age 10

Feelings are the sunshine and shadows of our mind that control the changeable climate of our moods. Helping children to cope with their feelings and emotional responses means helping them to become aware of their own feelings and the feelings of others. It also means helping them to express and control their feelings, and to understand and cope with the feelings of others.

A feeling is an internal reaction to something you experience (a stimulus). It has both physical and psychological effects. Different feelings have different physical symptoms - bodily changes including chemical processes, heart rate and muscle tensions. Psychological change comes from the interpretations we make of what we perceive or think which cause our consciousness to flood with emotion.

Primary emotions like fear, anger, and love can occur unconsciously. Complex emotions require processing in the mind. Sometimes we are conscious of emotion but not sure about what we are feeling. Often we are not aware of the origin of our feelings and when we do have an emotional response its purpose is to influence other people.

Feelings are infectious: they can directly influence how other people feel, and can signal what your needs are. Children are very honest in their expression of feelings. They do not tend to suppress them in the way adults do. They do not find it easy to control their feelings, and they are often not aware of the feelings of others.

One way to become more aware of the variety of human feelings is to list, with children, all the words we use to describe being happy, sad, angry, afraid or excited. Another way is to look at pictures showing a range of facial expressions of people and discuss what each may be feeling and why. Role play the physical, non-verbal indicators of feeling of gesture, posture and expression. Can children tell from a person's body language what their feelings might be, and why? Music is a strong communicator of feeling. Listen to music and discuss the feelings it conveys. Art also can convey emotion, as can stories and poems. What are the feelings being expressed? How do they make you feel? What do others feel?

The following starters for thinking encourage children to think about their own and others' feelings.

Thinking processes: Empathy, imagination, me-cognition

Links: About Me, p.14; 'Empathy (facial expressions)' in *Values for Thinking*, pp.57-9

Starters for thinking

- Make a list of all the different feelings you can think of. Arrange them into groups and explain why you grouped them that way.
- 'Happiness is ... '. Think of five or more ways to end this sentence.
- When do you feel lonely? What do you do to stop feeling lonely?
- How do you know when someone is feeling shy? How could you help them to stop being shy?
- 'Friendship is ... '. Think of five or more ways to end this sentence.
- 'Anger is ... '. Think of five or more ways to end this sentence.
- Design 'mood badges' that describe some of the different feelings or moods people have.
- Show a picture. Write about it in words or sentences. How does it make you feel?
- Use a candle to focus attention. Pause to reflect on a question, e.g. 'How do you feel today?'
- How has something you have said or done affected other people? How did they feel?
- What is your favourite place? Describe it and how it makes you feel.
- Why do people get cross? How can you help someone who is very cross?
- 'Fear is ... '. Think of five or more ways to end this sentence.
- Think and write about five things that make you feel good and say why.
- How might you cheer someone up who is feeling sad?
- What do you like (or love) and hate about holidays? (Or any other chosen subject)
- Write a note to say thank you to someone who has made you feel good. Say what they did and how it made you feel.
- 'Love is ... '. Think of five or more ways to end this sentence.

8 Green Thinking

'If we don't look after the world, who will?' Daniel, age 9

'Green thinking' means thinking about ways to preserve and enhance the environment. It is stimulated by engagement with real problems and lived experience and involves applying our knowledge and skills to improve the environment. Any local environment can offer starters for investigation, problem solving and 'green thinking'.

Questions to ask about any environment include:

- *What* – What are the problems? What do we need to find out? What should we do?
- *Where* – Where do the problems occur?
- *Why* – Why is it a problem?
- *When* – when do problems occur?
- *Who* – Who are involved?
- *How* – How can we improve the environment? Make it safer? Conserve it? Make it more beautiful?

Issues in the local environment that might be worth thinking about include:

Green spaces: how to use them, improve them; design a play area.

Keeping the neighbourhood tidy: how to discourage litter, encourage tidiness, design litter bins, where best to put them

Local routes: to places of interest – the quickest, the safest, the most interesting

Local transport: how it could be improved; the road, rail, sea or air transport of the future; consider speed, safety, payment and pollution factors

Local issues: what are the main local problems? What are the causes, and what the possible cures? What can you do about it? Have you any local contacts?

Conservation: what should be conserved, why, how, where, and when?

Old people: how to help them, how they can help us, problems of old age

Leisure facilities: how to design a leisure complex to include a wide range of activities that would appeal to local people

Recycling: what needs recycling, why and how

Campaigning: fundraise, make and advertise something to help the local environment

Find information on conservation and green issues in local newspapers or organisations. Focus on local needs and how they can be met, helping children to see where in a small way they can make a difference.

Thinking processes: Critical/creative thinking, problem posing, reasoning, evaluating

Links: Designing a Better World, p.22; Into the Future, p.32; Problem Solving, p.54; Thinking about School, p.60. See also 'Conservation' in *Poems for Thinking*, p.32; 'Respect for the Environment' in *Values for Thinking*, p.107

Starters for thinking

- What is pollution? What are the dangers of pollution?
- What are your views about graffiti?
- How would you improve a local park or green space?
- Design a safe but interesting play area for children.
- What are the problems with litter? How can we help? Design a litterbin that would help improve the environment.
- What problems do birds face? How can we help? Design a bird table that would help feed birds in winter.
- Where do all the puddles go?
- Design a poster to warn children about the dangers of smoking.
- How could local transport be improved?
- Design a leisure complex to include activities that would appeal to local people.
- What is the most serious problem the world faces today? Can you think of any solutions to this problem?
- Design a device for watering house plants while you are away.
- Design a garden to attract wildlife. Think of form, colour, and essentials such as water, sun.
- Create a poster or advert for a local green space or recycling centre.

9 How Many Uses?

'*There is always another use for anything.*' Ben, age 11

'What can you use it for?' is a common test of creativity. To use this technique, think of an item or object, usually a common one like a brick, paperclip, pencil, or bucket, and set the children the task of thinking of all the possible uses for that object, without being limited to what the object is normally used for, what it is called, or how it is usually thought of. For example, how many uses can you think of for a wellington boot in four minutes? The number of different ideas is said to provide an indicator to creativity in thinking.

'How many uses?' is a technique not just for testing, but also for practising and developing creative thinking. It helps develop fluency and flexibility of thinking, and to break out of fixed and limited ways of looking at things. One such limitation is the 'fallacy of the single function': that is, the mental habit of thinking that there is only one answer, only one way of looking at something or doing something, or only one use for anything. There is, as Ben says, always another idea or way of thinking that is possible if we are sufficiently creative.

Sometimes you may wish to set a time limit, such as three to five minutes; at other times set a quantity limit, such as 10, 20 or 50 uses.

For example: *What are the possible uses for a brick?*

Here are some ideas from a group of ten year olds.

A paper weight, a doorstop, a boat anchor, paint powder (crushed), shoe soles, a ruler, red chalk, a stop signal, a leaf press, a step, a stool, a target for shooting at, children's toy bricks, a weight, a boundary marker. How many ways are there to: build a wall, make a path, fill a hole, sand something, make a sign (using red letters), crack nuts?

You can ask children to identify their most creative idea (the one they think no-one else has thought of). You can make it into a scoring game, for example with one point for each idea and two points for an idea no one else has had.

Thinking processes: Creative thinking, imagination, hypothesising

Links: Designing a Better World, p.22; What If ... ?, p.68

Starters for thinking

How many uses can you think of for …

- a cardboard box?
- a towel?
- a nail?
- a spoon?
- a brick?
- a sheet of paper?
- a candle?
- old newspapers?
- rubber bands?
- a pencil?
- a marble?
- a button (or coin)?
- a plastic drinking glass?
- a paperclip?
- a piece of string?
- a shoe (or wellington boot)?
- a coathanger?
- a handkerchief?
- an old sock?
- a CD?

10 Into the Future

'*We are the future.*' Daniella, age 10

The twenty-first century demands increasing flexibility and imagination from our young people. The majority of children currently in primary school will enter careers that do not yet exist, and work in jobs that involve technology that has not yet been invented. They will not have one job for life but will change professions four or five times in their careers. It is estimated that information is doubling every three years. Children need an education that equips them with the skills they will need for an uncertain future. And their future will be a long one – as they can expect another eighty or more years of active life.

We are preparing them for many possible future worlds. For this they need the skills of 'possibility thinking', the ability to ask questions such as 'What if..?', 'Perhaps if ... ?' 'Why?' and 'Why not?' To help them we need to model these questions, and focus them on what concerns them all – the problems and opportunities of their future world.

How do we help to prepare them for this changing world? One way is to try to engage them in 'futures thinking' – to think ahead. We ask them to imagine what it might be like in a future world, for example to think about how things might change - what sort of jobs they will do, the kind of houses they will live in, how the environment may change, what inventions and new forms of travel there might be, what holidays they will take, or what the school of the future might be like.

One of the disquieting features of recent research into children's attitudes is the apparent growth in their fears about the future. How do we instil the confidence that they can make a difference? One way might be to ask them to imagine their ideal future world, and the ways in which this world might be realised.

The following starters are other ways of encouraging 'possibility thinking' about the future.

Thinking processes: Creative thinking, hypothesising, evaluating outcomes

Links: About Me, p.14; Green Thinking, p.28; What If ... ?, p.68

Starters for thinking

- Design a robot of the future that will make life easier. Explain how it works and what it can do.
- Design a new form of transport for the future.
- Plan an ideal classroom of the future.
- Design one thing that would improve the human body.
- Design a house of the future.
- What do you hope to do when you leave school? What do you need to do to achieve your ambition?
- What three wishes do you have for the future of the world? Why do you have these particular wishes?
- Design a school uniform or fashion item for the year 2060.
- If you were to become Prime Minister and could run the country, what changes would you make?
- Design a time capsule for someone in the future to find. What five things would you put in it and why?
- What is the greatest problem the world faces in the future? What possible solutions might there be?
- Design a room of the future that you would like to live in.
- What one discovery would most help the world in the future? Why?
- How might your life change in the future?

11 Make a List

'*Making a list is like putting your memory on paper.*' Sunil, age 8

One way to remember things is to make a list. We can organise a list by putting our ideas in groups or in a particular order. We remember best when information is put into a pattern or order. Lists are useful because our short term memory has a limited capacity and quickly becomes overloaded. A famous research article concluded that seven (plus or minus two) was the number of unconnected items, for example numbers, names or facts, that adults can successfully store in their short term memory. It is no surprise then that there are seven wonders of the world and seven days of the week, the Secret Seven and the Magnificent Seven, but not the Great Eight. Try remembering the whole of a large set, such as the names of the apostles: after seven (and sometimes before seven) remembering becomes difficult. Research this with your children.

Play memory games with your children, such as 'Memory' (a variation of Kim's game). In this game you make a list of ten simple words, and number them from one to ten. Read the list including the numbers out loud to the group. Can they remember the list of words? How many? Now say any number from one to ten. Who knows what word corresponds to the number on your list? Vary the game to include words about a topic you are studying, or ask children to compile their own memory lists to test others.

Ask the children who makes lists and why. Research the making of lists by hunting for examples in newspapers and magazines. Encourage them to make their own lists or memos of things to remember each day. What do you need to write down in case you forget? What lists do you make in your life? What are the important things to remember today?

The following starters explore further the making of lists to challenge thinking or to aid memory.

Thinking processes: Analysing, classifying, creative thinking, ordering, memorising

Links: About Me, p.14; Picture This, p.50; Thought Showers, p.63; Visualising, p.64. For more on memory games see *Games for Thinking* in this series.

Starters for thinking

- List the things you might give to a friend who is in hospital to cheer them **up.**
- Write down all the things you could do if you were bored.
- List as many things as you can that make you laugh.
- List all the things that are tools. Put them into groups.
- List things that are sticky (or made from wool, etc.). Put them into groups.
- List ten things you could fit into a matchbox.
- List all the things you might find on a beach (or in a kitchen, in a teacher's drawer etc.).
- List the best things in your life.
- List what you know about ... (a chosen topic).
- Make a list of things which begin with 'M'. Sort them into different groups.
- Make a list of things which end in 'K'. Sort them into different groups
- Can you list five things you know for certain? Five things you don't know? Five things you will never know?
- Make a list of excuses a child might give for being late to school.
- List 20 items of food or drink that people have for breakfast. What do you think would make the healthiest breakfast? (Choose up to five items.)
- List some new year's resolutions that would help you in the future.
- List everything you can which have wheels (or have legs).
- List as many things as you can made from wool (or other material e.g. wood).
- How many pairs? List things which go together, e.g. pepper and salt.
- List all the countries you can think of.
- List all the things you are good at. What are you best at? Why?
- What helps you to remember?

12 Meditation

'*Get your body calm and ready, get your thinking cap on steady!*' Cueing rhyme from Primary National Strategy (2005), 'Social and emotional aspects of learning'

There is growing interest in ways that meditation can enhance creativity, learning and the well-being of children – and for good reason. In an increasingly materialistic and competitive world many children are subject to the same stresses and strains as adults, becoming irritable, anxious and depressed. They are bombarded with information, images and noise. They are prey to the frustration and anger of others. They experience negative emotions more deeply and intensely than adults. They find it difficult to articulate their worries. Many lack concentration and are impulsive in their behaviour. Targets, tests and exams increase the pressure, with many children reporting sleepless nights over tests and other stresses in their lives.

We all need to develop calming-down strategies. To think or learn well, or cope with the challenges and frustrations of daily life, children need to learn to calm themselves. Meditation is one of the best ways of achieving a calm and receptive mind. Those who meditate regularly report that it can be deeply relaxing yet energising. It calms the mind, improves concentration, and boosts creativity. It can help reduce impulsivity and enhance self-esteem and self-awareness. It creates awareness of the silence within.

Forms of meditation have appeared in all major religions, as well as in yoga and other humanist traditions. However we do not need recourse to religious beliefs or to the value of developing spiritual awareness to justify the value of meditation. There are good reasons for including meditation as part of the daily experience of all children. Meditation helps to 'open the brain' and prepare the mind by focusing and energising it, getting it ready for the challenges of living and learning. It is an ideal starter for creative thinking – but how is it taught?

Most forms of meditation focus on:

- *posture* – body control
- *attention* – mind control
- *breathing* – breath awareness and control
- *concentration* – sustained attention
- *visualisation* – visualising images in the mind

A quiet space is necessary. Sometimes it can help to have a visual aid, for example a poster that all can see, or an object to hold such as a stone, shell, fir cone, piece of wood or fabric to focus on and try to keep the mind still. Using a chant or mantra can be very effective in stilling the mind. Any thinking lesson should include 'thinking time', moments of quiet meditation (sitting in silence for half a minute). If children do not experience these with teachers at school, when will they experience them?

Thinking processes: Focused attention, me-cognition, visualisation

Links: Visualisation, p.64

Starters for thinking

- Sit in the 'concentration position' – sit up, with head up, straight back and open chest to allow deep regular breathing. Count your breaths. Breathe deeply – in and out five times.
- Inhale fully and slowly and exhale fully and quickly; then reverse this – breathe in fully and quickly and breathe out slowly.
- Practise 'butterfly breathing'. Interlace your fingers and tuck them under your chin. Breathe in. Let your elbows come up and your head tilt back. Breathe out slowly and bring your elbows down.
- Calm yourself completely. Repeat 'Be calm ... be calm ... be calm.'
- Tense then relax your muscles. Be aware of every part of your body.
- Sit in silence, feeling your pulse.
- Sit in silence listening to distant sounds for ... (e.g. one minute).
- Ask children to visualise an orange in their mind. Focus on the orange. Slowly peel the orange (in their mind), looking carefully at details. 'Eat' a segment of orange. Focus on smell, touch, taste.
- Concentrate by focusing on an image ... (a picture, e.g. sea, sky, tree).
- Concentrate by focusing on an object ... (such as a leaf, candle or stone).
- Concentrate by focusing on a sound ... (a sound effect such as the sea, repeated musical sound or calming piece of music).
- Concentrate by focusing on a taste ...
- Concentrate by focusing on a smell ... (e.g. a perfumed candle).
- Concentrate by focusing on a word. Choose a word to chant with the children, preferably something calming like 'think', 'clear' or 'still'. Get the class to chant the word over and over again to clear and focus the mind.
- What strategies can you think of for calming down? Design a poster to help others to calm down.
- What is the value of meditation? Could it help you with your work or your life? How?

13 Music for Thinking

'Music is a kind of language that you can't quite understand. Sometimes talking about it helps you understand.' Amy, age 10

Music is a source of metaphysical conundrums. What is music? What does it do? What does it mean? Music raises questions that can provide a stimulus for aesthetic, musical and philosophical discussion with people of all ages. It has long been thought to be 'the medicine of the mind', not so much concerned with our physical as with our spiritual and psychological well-being. It is a unique tool for arousing our physical, emotional and intellectual faculties.

Music starts with listening. Yet we are so surrounded by noise that we block out much that we might listen to. We listen to significant sounds but ignore the rest. Children today are submerged in a sea of technological sound. No wonder teachers report that young children find attentive listening so difficult to achieve.

Music binds us in a special way to our social and cultural context, but children can easily be trapped in their own musical tastes and culture. Discussing music can be liberating when it shows other ways to think, feel and experience the sounds we hear. Musical enquiry can free children from simplistic and stereotypical responses to what they hear and so expand the mind.

Help them to think about the rich variety of sounds in their environment, including musical sounds. Using music as starters for thinking encourages attentive listening, discussing and responding to patterns of sounds. Explore musical sounds, and the place and value of music in human experience, as well as intellectual and emotional responses to music.

Sounds and silence are the raw materials of music. Some children have little or no experience of silence. In terms of music education listening to silence is as important as listening to music. The following are some starters for thinking about the intervals of sound and silence in music.

Thinking processes: Analysing, attentive listening, creative thinking

Links: Meditation, p.36; Visualising, p.64

Starters for thinking

- Which sounds are musical and which are not musical?
- Make a list of all the places where you hear music. Which place do you like best?
- What would the world be like without music?
- (*Play some music.*) Listen carefully to the music. What does the music make you think and feel? Write about your ideas.
- (*Play some orchestral music.*) Listen carefully to the music. List all the instruments you can hear. What does the music make you think of?
- If you were making a CD of your favourite music, with ten tracks, what would you choose to include?
- If you could play one musical instrument really well, which would you choose and why?
- List as many musical instruments as you can think of. Put them into four groups.
- Think of a tune you know well. Make up words to the tune to advertise the benefits of healthy eating.
- Design a new musical instrument. Describe the sounds it makes.
- Invent a story about how people first began to make music. What do you think the first musical instrument was?
- Make up a rap or song about people in your family.
- Why do people like to listen to music or learn to play an instrument?
- Make up a rap or song about showing respect to people (or the environment).
- (*Play some instrumental music.*) Close your eyes and listen carefully to the music. What pictures do you see in your mind? Draw the ideas, images or patterns that you see.
- What do you think are the most beautiful sounds in the world?
- (*Play some slow or sad music.*) Close your eyes and listen carefully to the music. Use words or drawings to describe your feelings, ideas, or images.
- (*Play some music from a different culture.*) What does this music make you think or feel? Write or draw your ideas.

14 Mysteries

'A mystery is something puzzling ... like why is there always one sock missing?' Fran, age 10

The world is full of unexplained things, words and events. Some of these mysteries are part of everyday life and have a simple explanation. Others are more complex and are open to different possible solutions. Some mysteries will, for one reason or another, never be answered.

Life is full of puzzles, and this must be so because human knowledge and understanding is incomplete. Science has made huge strides but there are many mysteries to be solved. A starting point might be to ask children: 'What do we not know about the world?' Here are some answers given by children:

We don't know how the world was created.

We don't know how to cure everyone of cancer.

Who built Stonehenge?

Does the Loch Ness monster really exist?

Is there life in outer space?

The philosopher Wittgenstein said: 'The true mystery of the world is the visible not the invisible.' There are many natural wonders in the world which puzzle the mind. There are historical mysteries that have baffled men in the past like the mystery of the *Marie Celeste*, mythical monsters like the Yeti, and mysterious phenomena like people who claim to foretell the future but can't say how. There are stories made up about mysteries by writers like Agatha Christie. There are poems about mysteries such as T.S. Eliot's 'Macavity the Mystery Cat' and there are the 'mystery plays' from the Middle Ages.

A characteristic of a mystery is that we are working with incomplete knowledge, and that one or more hypotheses may offer possible solutions. To the question 'Why is the sky blue?' one child responded: 'Perhaps God did not make it green in case it confused the animals.'

The following are some mysteries to stimulate thinking.

Thinking processes: Questioning, creative thinking, reasoning, evaluating

Links: Questions for Thinking, p.56; What Do You Think?, p.66

Starters for thinking

- What are mysteries? Can you give some examples?
- Do you think there is life on other planets? Give reasons why there might be and why there might not be.
- Why are people different?
- What do we not know about the world? Can you think of five or more things that we do not know the answer to?
- Are there such things as ghosts?
- Why are objects the colour they are? (Choose object and colour)
- Why do vegetables not grow in square shapes?
- (*Think of a mystery person.*) Who am I thinking of? (Children ask relevant questions to find out who this person is. Teacher can only answer 'Yes' or 'No'.) Play with a partner.
- 'A bird in the hand is worth two in a bush.' What does this proverb mean? Can you give an example?
- (*Show a mystery object, e.g. an old shoe, a bag. Ask questions such as:*) Where was this found? Who does it belong to? What's special about it?
- Who owns the water we drink?
- Mystery character (or animal): Choose a character or animal. Describe your life without saying who or what you are. Others can then question you, and try to guess who you are.
- Why do people say: 'Elephants never forget'? Why do elephants never forget?
- Why do dogs' tails wag and other animals' tails do not?
- Why do we measure time?
- How high can a cat jump?
- Why do midges only bite some people?
- Why is water clear?
- Will we ever have all the answers to all questions (or mysteries)?

15 News Stories

'*Why is there so much bad news and so little good news?*' Paula, age 9

There are six questions that journalism students are taught to answer somewhere in their news articles to check that they have covered the whole story. These questions can stimulate creative thinking about any idea or topic by encouraging you to view it from various angles.

1 *Who?* (Characters) Who is involved? What are the people aspects of the story? Who did it, will do it?
2 *What?* (Acts) What happened? What should happen? What were the results?
3 *When?* (Time) When did, will, should this happen?
4 *Where?* (Scene) Where did, will, should this happen? Where else? What is the effect of this location on the action, characters?
5 *Why?* (Purpose) Why did this happen? Why should it be done, avoided, permitted?
6 *How?* (Method) How did it happen? How can it be described, understood? How did beginning lead to conclusion?

Some teachers invite children to bring in, discuss and display their favourite newspaper stories, or have a 'News board' where children can display news items of interest. This might include the latest news, local news or school news. In these classrooms 'What's in the news today?' is a question that can always be answered. An important element of children choosing their own news stories is that they will be relevant to their own lives and interests. The teachers can also broaden their horizons with relevant news from around the world. Collecting newspapers and magazines from around the world could be a focus for ongoing research, as could a survey of newspapers read at home.

Creating a class newspaper or online news service could provide other starters for thinking. Interviewing local journalists, visiting the local newspaper or news station or other forms of reporting would create good opportunities for devising questions and presenting news to others. Another stimulus for thinking is to put news headline on the board for children to create their own news stories round.

Children could research and discuss the different sections of a newspaper and different types of features and news reports, leading with older children to the question 'If you were to edit a newspaper, what sections would you include?'

The following starters for thinking draw upon childrens' innate interest in the world of imagination and reality that they find in news and stories.

Thinking processes: Analysing, creative thinking, information processing, evaluating

Links: Mysteries, p.40; What Do You Think?, p.66. See also www.newswise.com

Starters for thinking

- Invent a news story about an alien visiting the earth.
- Think of some really good news. Write a short report of it. Then share it with someone, then move and tell someone else that news.
- Invent an amazing news story connected with the colour red.
- (*Give each child a random object from a special box e.g. piece of material, foil, paper.*) What is this? How might it have been important in a news story?
- Write the beginning of a news story for the children to create their own endings to the story.
- 'Dinosaur discovered!' Write a news story to go with this headline.
- Make up a story which contains these three words ... (random words, e.g. feather, helmet, elephant).
- What one piece of advice would give to a young child? What other advice? (Advice column).
- Amazing underwater discovery! Write the news story.
- Create an interesting problem that you would like a newspaper or magazine to answer for you? (Share and discuss these).
- A message has been found in a bottle? What does it say? What is the story?
- Can you make up a story where there was good news followed by bad news, then good news, then bad news, etc.? ('Fortunately ... unfortunately ... etc.)
- Invent a story about ... (a strange character, e.g. Foolish Jack, Mr. Knowall). What might they have done?
- What's the story? (*Hand two headlines from a newspaper to every child*). Create a news story to go with the chosen headline.

16 Number Puzzler

'*If numbers make you numb what do more numbers make you?*' Child, age 10

We are all born with a number sense - a region in the human brain that acts like a primitive calculator, and gives us the ability to use and understand numbers. This part of the brain is located in the inferior parietal cortex just above and behind each ear. Babies are born with a rudimentary understanding of number and the logic of identity (for example that 1 is 1 not 2), but it takes years for this innate number sense to develop into an understanding of numerical calculations.

This number sense is a fundamental aspect of mathematical intelligence. It gives a child the ability to understand numbers and, through the system of numeration, the power to describe the world with numbers. The system of numeration we use derives from an ancient Hindu system, further developed by Arab traders in the tenth century who introduced the zero. The economy of the Hindu-Arabic system enables all numbers to be represented by a finite set of digits: 0123456789. The ancient Egyptians needed 15 symbols to write the number 366, the Romans needed seven, but our Hindu-Arabic system needs only three.

Our system uses ten as a base and each digit is understood as a number according to its place (each place being multiplied by the power of ten). The trouble with our system is that place value is such a hard concept to grasp. Young children more easily think of numbers as quantities. Older children more naturally think of numbers visually on a line. They need time to explore number patterns and operations and to experiment with their own methods and ways of representing numbers through diagrams, symbols and lines.

Number puzzles give children the chance to experiment with creating their own strategies. The ways children tackle the puzzles gives concrete evidence of their mathematical thinking. If the puzzles are challenging, yet within a child's capability, they develop the capacity for logical and numerical thinking. They can also make working with numbers fun.

The following number puzzles can be adapted to suit a range of ages and abilities. They can first be considered individually then tackled in pairs or small groups. Encourage your children then to create and experiment with their own puzzles.

Thinking processes: Logical/numerical thinking, creative thinking, reasoning

Links: Creative Shapes, p.20

Starters for thinking

- What are numbers? (Where can you see numbers?)
- The answer is 12. What might the question be?
- Make up five word problems for a given calculation e.g. 21 – 14
- Put ten random numbers on the board. Ask children to study them and see what links they can find between them (patterns, order, calculations etc).
- Work out how many months (days/hours/minutes) there are until your next birthday.
- How many different ways could you make £2.00 using coins? Which would be heaviest to carry to the shops?
- Using the digits 1, 2, 3, 4, 5, how many different numbers can you make?
- How many number calculations can you think of where the answer is 25? (use + – × ÷)
- Choose two digits between 1 and 9. Try to make all the numbers from 1-20 or more using only these digits and + – × ÷.
- I send birthday cards to 5 people and they all send birthday cards to each other. How many birthday cards have been sent? Make up another puzzle like this.
- Take a sequence of numbers, e.g. 10, 100, 25, 49, 16, and write a chain to link them (e.g. 10 × 10 ÷ 4 + 45 – 29).
- Can you make every number from 1 – 20 using only four 4s and mathematical symbols? What other numbers can you make using four 4s? (Which can't you make? Why not?)
- A café has tables with four legs, and stools with three legs. There are 42 furniture legs altogether – how many tables and stools might there be?
- 'I am thinking of a number. What is it? You have ten questions. I can only answer yes or no.' Try this with a partner.
- Imagine you are a number, e.g. 8. Tell me all you know about yourself, and what you can do.
- In a barn there are 4 heads and 12 legs altogether. How many cows and hens are in the barn? (Try alternatives, e.g. a barn with 30 heads and 68 feet!)
- How many four-digit numbers can you make using the digits in the number 1945? Put them in order, biggest to smallest.

17 Odd One Out

'*We are all odd in some way or other*.' Janie, age 11

'Odd One Out' is a good strategy for developing reasoning, critical and creative thinking skills. A child is presented with three things and asked which is the odd one out. Here there are no right or wrong answers, but a number of possibilities to think about and analyse. The process of reasoning and justification is the point of this activity. The child must answer the question: 'Why is this the odd one out?' They must give reasons to justify their choices. They must also be open-minded to other possibilities. They should be asked to consider, 'Could it be a different one?' The answer to this is always yes, for there are many ways we can analyse the factors and variables that make up the potential similarities and differences between things.

'Odd One Out' can be used to identify pupils' understanding of key concepts in different subjects. In a numeracy lesson a teacher might put three numbers on the board, such as 9, 5 and 10; or in science three materials; or in English three characters to compare and contrast – then ask the children to choose the 'odd one out' and to give a reason. For example: which shape is the odd one out of these shapes?

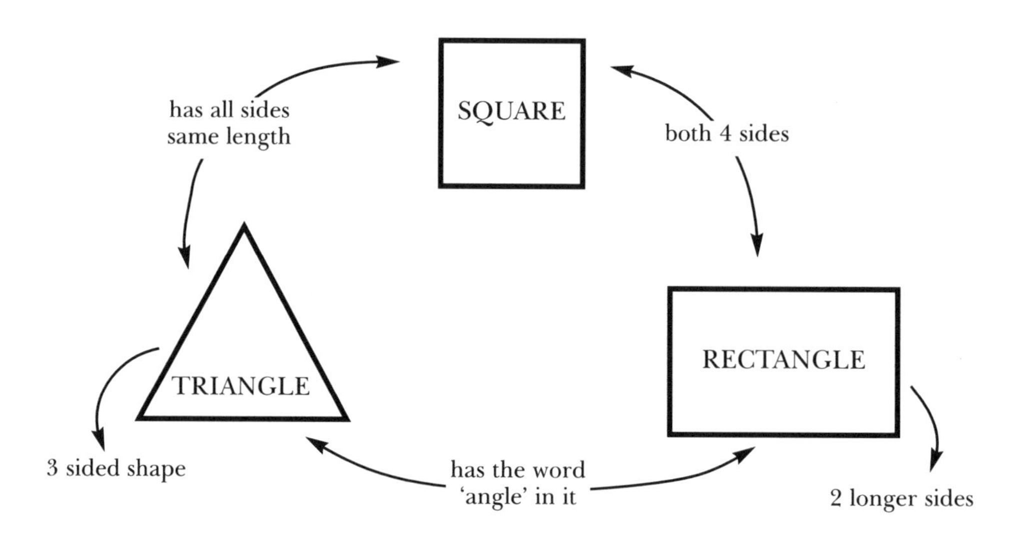

Teachers who use this strategy claim it can reveal gaps in the knowledge and vocabulary that the children are able to use. The children think of it as a game and can think of examples and ideas in different curriculum subjects.

Can you think of three or more things, words, objects or people, and give reasons why one, two or each of them might be the odd one out?

Thinking processes: Classifying, comparing, reasoning

Links: PMI, p.52; Similar and Different, p.58; Would You Rather ... ?, p.72

Starters for thinking

Which of these could be the odd one out? Give reasons for your answer.

- fish, bird, frog
- bus, car, lorry
- rabbit, duck, snake
- cotton, wool, nylon
- wood, seeds, trees
- 9, 5,10 (or 36, 11, 25 etc.)
- square, triangle, rectangle
- sun, moon, stars
- black, white, grey
- Easter egg, duck egg, football
- horse, snake, beetle, worm
- violin, drum, flute
- silk, leather, fur
- true, good, beautiful
- police officer, fire officer, hospital worker
- Spain, France, Germany, England
- Make up your own 'Odd One Out' puzzle, with possible answers for it.

18 Philosophical Questions

'Philosophy is the way you sort out problems in life when nobody knows the answer.' Simon, age 11

'All people by nature desire to know,' said Aristotle, and the way children find out is to ask questions. Some of these questions such as 'Why doesn't the sky fall on our heads?' 'Why do cows eat grass?' 'How old is the cat?' are questions about the physical world. Other questions are not about the physical world, but about our ideas (or concepts) of the world, about what we think and believe. With some of these questions, such as 'Why are people cruel to each other?' 'Does God exist?' 'What is love?' the right answer may not be known, or there may be several possible answers. These questions arise out of a child's natural curiosity, but they are not scientific. There is no one right answer, but many possible answers and viewpoints. They are questions about what we think as human beings, and are about the way we make sense of life. These kinds of questions are philosophical.

Philosophy differs from science, maths and other forms of understanding, in that it relies not on things in the world but on our thoughts about the world. Philosophical thinking is necessary because words and ideas can confuse the human mind and meanings can be manipulated. To become critical, creative and caring citizens, children will need the confidence to question what they see and hear, the skills to think and reason for themselves, and the creativity to try to work things out when they don't know the answer.

Asking and answering philosophical questions is where philosophy begins. Key questions at the heart of philosophy include:

- *What does this mean?*
- *Is it true?*
- *How do we know?*

Children bring with them into the world elastic minds capable of being stretched in all sorts of directions and an ability to ask not only everyday questions like 'Where's my food?' but also deep and challenging questions like the following questions from four year olds: 'Why do people die?' 'Why do chickens lay eggs?' and 'How does an oak tree fit into an acorn?' This curiosity is early evidence of philosophical intelligence.

The following questions are some starters to stimulate children's philosophical thinking.

Thinking processes: Questioning, reasoning, creative thinking, evaluating

Links: Questions for Thinking, p.56; What Do You Think?, p.66; What If ... ?, p.68. For more on philosophy with children see www.sapere.co.uk

Starters for thinking

- Is an apple dead or alive?
- How do you know you are not dreaming at this moment?
- How do you know when something is true or not true?
- Is it right to eat animals?
- What is the difference between pretending and lying?
- What is the difference between a real person and a robot?
- Is there a difference between your mind and your brain?
- Can animals think?
- Is it ever right to tell lies?
- What are the most valuable things in your life?
- If you swapped brains with someone else would you be a different person?
- What is the difference between magic and science?
- What are the most important rights of children?
- What goes on forever? What does 'forever' mean?
- Why did God not make us perfect?
- If you fail, does it mean you are a failure? Why?
- What are thoughts? How do they affect us?
- What is evil? Are some people born evil?
- How did the world begin?
- Is it ever right to steal?
- What does it mean to be good? Is it better to be good or happy?
- What happens to you when you die?
- What is a problem? Does every problem have a solution? Why? Give an example.
- Is there only one true religion? Could many religions be true?
- Do you think there is a heaven? Why?

19 Picture This

'*I am a visual learner.*' Sasha, age 10

We live in an age of visual images. In industrial societies, most people spend much of their time looking at television screens, web graphics, print illustrations, and other types of visual displays. Because of this, many would argue that we need a more visually oriented educational system, one focused more directly on 'visual literacy' - the ability to understand and to produce visual messages.

Many children have a preference for visual learning, and would benefit from a more visually oriented curriculum. All children need to learn to how to create and read visual meaning, not just to consume it. Central to the skills of visual thinking are the capabilities to perceive the visual world accurately and to recreate aspects of one's visual experience, even in the absence of relevant physical stimuli.

Picasso once said he wished he could draw as well as a child. The beauty of a young child's drawing is that it is unconstrained. They will quite happily redesign the human body, the family car or the local school. Offer children a random arrangement of lines and they will soon start to pick out significant patterns and pictorial possibilities. Ask children to draw a number of dots on a piece of paper and see how they create a design or picture by connecting the dots or incorporating them in some overall scheme. A generous supply of coloured pens can offer a wealth of creative opportunities.

Show a 'picture of the week'. Ask children to write thoughts or questions about the picture. Put these on a chart or make them into a booklet. Discuss them at the end of the week. Share and discuss with others questions about the visual arts, for example: Why do people make art? Can a painting be a better image of something (or someone) than a photograph?

The following are some starters to stimulate visual thinking.

Thinking processes: Creative thinking, imagining, spatial thinking, visualising

Links: Creative Shapes, p.20; Designing a Better World, p.22

Starters for thinking

- Design your own cartoon character. Tell a story about your character.
- Draw a plan of your bedroom or of how you would like your bedroom to be.
- Draw a map to show where a pirate has hidden his treasure. Give clues or directions on how to find the treasure.
- Draw a sentence using a picture for each word. Can someone else understand what it says?
- Draw a plan of your ideal house. Show what each room is used for.
- Make a mind map showing different kinds of animals.
- Imagine a new species of fish (or bird) has been discovered. Draw and describe it.
- Make a mind map showing different kinds of sports.
- What might a being from another planet look like? Draw and describe it.
- (*Draw a picture on the board, e.g. an ink blot.*) What do you think this is? Draw and write about what you think it might be. What could this shape be?
- Can you depict an emotion, for example anger or happiness, using only colours, lines and marks?
- Invent and draw a new poisonous flower. Name it and write some information about it: where was it found? Who found it? What does it smell of? Is it poisonous? What does it look like?
- Invent and draw a badge, crest or shield for you or your family.
- Every clown has a different face. (*Show an example.*) Make up your own clown face design.
- (*Draw a common object, e.g. a pair of scissors*). Can you change this into something different? Draw and describe what you could change it to.
- Draw you and your family or the people you live with at home.
- What is your favourite picture? Can you draw your version of your favourite picture?
- Draw an upside down picture of a friend (or of a given image).

20 Plus, Minus and Interesting

'*Sometimes it's hard to think of interesting things.*' Tasmin, age 8

'Think before you leap,' says Edward de Bono, and Plus, Minus and Interesting (PMI) is a strategy which aims to compel thinking about any situation before coming to a judgement about it. The process involves listing all the good points, bad points and interesting points about a given idea, object or event. It is one of the most effective tools for directing attention and generating thinking about different aspects of a topic.

Plus relates to the positive elements of the topic, Minus to the negative elements, and Interesting to those points are neither good or bad, but are regarded as neutral observations, comments or points of interest:

'*I'm not sure about this. Let's do a PMI.*'

'*To find out more about what we think, let's do a PMI.*'

'*There are two options. Let's do a PMI on each*'

PMI is a useful evaluation tool that can be used to generate thinking about any situation or piece of work. Pictures, objects or texts can be subjected to creative analysis using the PMI method.

Make a list for each category of good points under Plus, bad points under Minus, and neutral but relevant under Interesting about a given topic. For example, think about what you have done today, yesterday or during the last week. What were the positive, negative and interesting points in your life during this time? Or choose a book, picture or TV film and do a PMI on it.

A PMI analysis can be done on topics across the curriculum. Children can choose their own topics, issues or events for a PMI. The following are examples of activities with which to practise divergent thinking using PMI.

Thinking processes: Analysing, classifying, creative thinking, reasoning, evaluating

Links: Make a List, p.34; What Do You Think?, p.66; Would You Rather ... ?, p.72

Starters for thinking

List the plus points, minus points and interesting points ...

- If you could live forever.
- If everyone looked the same.
- If you shared your house with your friends instead of your parents.
- If television had never been invented.
- If children did not have to attend school unless they wanted to.
- If people had to wear badges to show what mood they were in.
- If seats were taken out of buses.
- If you were a superhero.
- If you were invisible.
- If you were born in ... (e.g. Ancient Egypt)
- If you won a fortune on the lottery.
- If you could see into the future.

- Choose a book (or film, TV programme etc.) you have read and do a PMI on it.
- Do a PMI about today (or yesterday, or last weekend).
- Do a PMI about your school.

21 Problem Solving

'*Why is there always another problem?*' Kate, age 8

Life is full of problems, as Kate says, and they seem never-ending. Kate's ability to solve problems will be the key to her success in life. Problems can stimulate and develop the skills of thinking and reasoning, draw on knowledge and experience and help build confidence and capability. Having a problem is a good starter for thinking.

Real-life problems tend to be ill-defined and multi-faceted - how to resolve a quarrel between two people, buy a new house, or decide on a career. Such problems rarely have a single or final solution. They are open-search problems in which there is no one method which will guarantee the right answer, only a variety of possible approaches from which we choose a 'best fit' solution. The solution does not necessarily end the process, but often reveals further problems.

Identify a real-life problem from your own experience, or ask children to share a problem they have experienced, for example what to do if they want to buy something and do not have the money. Share this problem with a child or group of children, expressing the problem at the child's level of understanding. Ask the children to suggest what they could do to solve the problem, or make a plan by which the problem could be solved.

What children need are some problem solving strategies to help in this process. The following questions were devised and used by a group of children to help solve their problems:

- *What is my problem?* – formulating the problem
- *How can I explain it?* – explaining the problem
- *What can I do about it?* – devising courses of action
- *Which way is best?* – decision making
- *How can I do it?* – implementing a solution

One way is to discuss plans to overcome problems in the real world. Another resource for discussion is favourite stories. Many stories that we share with children have a problem element which can be found in the theme or plot. What problem(s) does the hero/heroine face? What would the children do if they were the character in the story? How might the problem be solved?

Problem solving skills are developed through tackling a wide range of problems. The following are some starters for thinking about problems.

Thinking processes: Creative thinking, problem posing, reasoning, evaluation

Links: Designing a Better World, p.22; What Do You Think?, p.66; Would You Rather ... ?, p.72

Starters for thinking

- What is a problem? Give examples. What is your recipe for solving problems?
- What is your recipe for a happy class? Write a list of ingredients and your method for using them to create a happy class. (See example on p.11.)
- What causes fights between people? What can help prevent fights?
- How might the problems of too much traffic on the roads be solved?
- Write a recipe for being a good friend (write a list of ingredients and your method for being a good friend).
- Many people are dying of hunger in the world. How could we help?
- What is your recipe for keeping healthy?
- Many people are homeless. How should they be helped?
- What would you put into an emergency aid pack to help people made homeless in an earthquake?
- How could the richer countries help people in poorer countries? Should they? Why?
- Write a recipe for a healthy sandwich. List the ingredients and instructions on how to make it.
- Write the steps you would take to help resolve an argument or fight between children in school. What is your recipe for resolving conflicts?
- A friend of yours has been upset by someone calling her names. What might you do to sort out the problem?
- Design an emergency shelter for people made homeless in a disaster.
- Design something that would help someone get up in the morning.
- You want to buy a present for a friend's birthday but don't have enough money. What could you do?
- What are the most important problems we have to solve in the world?

22 Questions for Thinking

'Where does the question mark come from?' Ravi, age 10

Questioning lies at the heart of learning and teaching. Teachers help children learn by asking good questions, and by encouraging them to ask their own questions. Children should have opportunities to generate questions, and their ability to do so will improve with practice. In an enquiring classroom, good questions, from teachers and children, are valued and displayed.

Give children a common object such as a chair or cup and ask them to list as many questions about the object as they can. Another way is to ask children to generate questions on a chosen topic or text individually, then in twos or larger groups. Share and analyse questions together. How many different questions were developed? Discuss the kinds of questions that were asked. What were the most interesting questions? What made them interesting?

A range of questions can be asked about any event, picture or object, for example a teapot. How much does it hold? What is it made from? Why is it that shape? How does it retain heat? Is it a good design? What is its purpose? Does it fit its purpose? Is it beautiful? How was it made? How old is it? Where was it made? How much did it cost? Is it good value? Who has owned/owns it? What do you think of it? How might its design be improved? and so on.

Albert Einstein once said: 'The important thing is not to stop questioning.' Questions, like good wine, can improve with keeping. Display them, savour them, come back to them. Find some more. Sort them into categories, for example:

- questions we can answer
- questions we can find the answer for
- questions that cannot be answered.

Discuss with children the nature of questions. Give them a list of questions and ask which they think is the best or most interesting question. Discuss good and bad questions. Find out what questions they would like to have answered. Display the question of the day for children to see at the start of the day. Use think/pair/share. Give children time to think about the question (or draft responses), discuss with a partner then share and discuss as a whole group. Decide on someone to interview, for example a visitor or a local VIP. Ask students to devise, share, evaluate and prioritise the best interview questions.

Thinking processes: Questioning, evaluating. hypothesising, reasoning

Links: Philosophical Questions, p.48; What Do You Think?, p.66; What If ...?, p.68. See also 'Why?', *First Poems for Thinking*, p.70; 'Thinking about questions', *Poems for Thinking*, p.74; 'Thinking about questions', *Stories for Thinking*, p.86, in this series.

Starters for thinking

- What is a question? Why ask questions?
- How many questions can you think of to ask about a chair? (*Show a chair.*)
- How many questions can you think of to ask about this object … (*Show an object.*)
- Write ten questions to ask this person … (*name a person they all know*) if you were to interview them.
- 'I wonder why …' Think of five or more ways to end this sentence.
- Make up ten good questions about … (*choose a topic you are studying*).
- Think of ten questions for which the answer is 'My house.'
- Write down all the questions you can think of which have the answer … (e.g. '24').
- How many questions can you think of where the answer is 'green'?
- How many maths questions can you ask to investigate this room (or e.g. a piece of clothing)?
- Why do leopards have spots? (or zebras stripes, etc.)
- Why do we use cutlery? (Design and draw your own cutlery.)
- Use a candle to focus attention, and create a pause to reflect on a question, e.g. 'What would you like to ask God?' (or 'What would you like to find out?')
- Show a globe. Ask children to brainstorm questions to ask about the planet. Share and discuss.
- What mathematical questions can you ask about an object?
- What question would you most like answered? (Pass this to a friend to answer!)

23 Similar and Different

'What is the difference between 100 real and 100 imaginary dollars?' Immanuel Kant

Comparing and contrasting are the basic building blocks of thinking. Noting sameness and difference are the foundations of human cognition, and all reasoning depends on these skills. Psychologists who wish to assess a child's level of reasoning use tests which requires a child to look for similarities and differences between two objects. Acts of comparing and contrasting enable children to relate one experience to another, to classify concepts, and to build a coherent and inter-connected picture of the world.

We help to sharpen children's perception through close observation and analysis. Take any two similar objects, for example two leaves, stones or potatoes, and challenge children to spot the differences. They should be able to observe and identify similarities, for example between two chairs which look almost but not quite the same. The child's conceptual development relies not just on recognising but also on defining similarities and differences. Perceptions need to be communicated through precise language. Scientific analysis of properties and classifications of natural objects depend on the use of these skills.

What is needed is not for the child simply to look, but to look and think. They can be helped to closely observe by being asked to draw from real life or from memory (and to compare the two). Always give children sufficient time. Help them to notice details, to look from different angles to compare features, to look at similarities and differences, and to see what changes are wrought over time.

Children can be asked to compare and contrast two real objects, or pictures of two objects or two named objects. They can practise doing this by listing what is similar and what is different. 'Similar' does not have to be identical but should have one or more shared variables. They can be asked to analyse what is similar and different in two pictures, places, times, events, texts and so on. We force them to think when we get them to choose and say why. They can also be asked which they prefer and why. Their judgements should be based on analysis of evidence and the giving of reasons.

The following starters for thinking ask children to compare and contrast various entities. They can also be asked to state which they prefer and why.

Thinking processes: Analysing, comparing, contrasting, categorising

Links: Make a List, p.34; Picture This, p.50; PMI, p.52

Starters for thinking

How are these objects similar? How are they different? Which do you prefer? Why?

- Jelly and ice cream
- A guitar and a vacuum cleaner
- A tree and a book
- A bus and a bicycle
- A boy and a dog
- A table and a chair
- Night and day
- A poem and a story
- A photograph and a painting
- A piece of music and the sound of bird song
- Spring and summer
- A dance and a race
- Two similar real objects, e.g. stones, feathers, seeds, fruits, vegetables, flowers
- Two photographs of the same scene, object or person, taken over time.
- Two pieces of music
- Two works of art
- Two characters in a book
- Two stories or poems
- Two events or places
- Two children in the class

24 Thinking About School

'*Your problems really begin when you go to school.*' Kulwinder, age 10

We all face problems in school, whether as children, teachers, non-teaching staff, parents or governors. School is a place where problem posing and problem solving take place on a daily basis. How we face the real problems of school can have immediate, practical effects on our lives. Identifying and trying to solve problems in school can really challenge children's thinking.

When a teacher asked her class to write down the real problems they faced in school, they identified a range of problems: bullying, cloakroom trouble, swearing in the playground, spitting in the playground, football at playtime, litter, not enough to do, shoes being hidden, mud, writing on walls. Thinking about the problems they faced as individuals, writing them down and sharing them, was the start. They then chose five issues to investigate in groups as an action research project and produced some practical solutions.

The range of school issues to think about is wide, including:

What school would I like? – facilities, equipment, children, teachers, activities

What school rules? – invent rules for children/teachers

What punishments are needed? – are they fair? ways of preventing unfairness

What school-day problems are there? – timing, timetable needed?

How to advertise your school – create an advert for your school/class/teacher

Directions – routes round the school, how to find way round (signs, maps)

How to improve open spaces – field, sports pitch, garden, new facilities e.g. pond

Playground – design/make play equipment, painted designs, teaching aids

Play problems – how to stop accidents e.g. dangerous games, how to prevent upsets/quarrels/bullying – divided areas? Different play times? Monitors?

School uniform – should there be one? Problems, designs?

School meals – problems, menus (healthy eating) how best timed, served, cost?

Classroom organisation – seating arrangements, storage, display. What the class lacks, how it could be better organised

Disabled facilities – wheelchairs, problems, solution

Library – type of books, shelf space, rota of visits, tidiness, problems

Sports Day – when, what races, refreshments, equipment, points or teams? What if it rains, what if there's an injury?

School play/production – what type, who will take part, audience, programme, whether to charge, seating, invitations, adverts

Parents evening – how might children organise, run and advertise this?

School fundraising – for charity, for school funds, for special people?

Thinking processes: Creative thinking, evaluating, information processing, questioning, reasoning

Links: Designing a Better World, p.22; Problem Solving, p.54; Questions for Thinking, p.56

Starters for thinking

- Why are we in school?
- Draw a map of your school. Label all the rooms.
- What would happen if there was no school?
- Design something to improve your playground.
- School rules: invent rules for children/teachers. Which are most important?
- Make up an advert for your school/class/teacher.
- Design a healthy menu for school meals for a week.
- What should children wear to go to school? Should there be school uniform? Design your ideal school uniform.
- Could this classroom be better organised? What does it lack?
- Make a mind map showing all the important features of your school.
- How could we improve the library?
- If we were to have a sports day, what would be your ideal school sports day?
- If you were the headteacher, how would you improve the school? (Think about people, buildings, play areas, lessons etc.)
- Make up a song about your school, using a well-known tune or your own tune.
- Is homework a good thing? Why? What kinds of homework are best?
- Make a list of what you like about school and a list about what you do not like about school. What could you do about some things you do not like?
- What is your favourite playground game? Say why.
- Invent a playground game with a goal, rules and purpose. (Suggest a few items of equipment.)
- Should children learn Latin (or any other foreign language)? Why?
- What would you teach if you were the teacher?
- Where would you like to take children on a school trip, and why?
- Is spelling important (or maths, science, music, art etc.)? Why?
- What would be a good motto for the school? Design a badge with this motto.

25 Thought Showers

'You have to go through a lot of ideas before you have a good idea.' Jerry, age 10

Thought showers, or brainstorming, are a common technique for generating ideas. Here the emphasis is on fluency – having as many ideas as possible.

Brainstorming is an idea-generating technique. Its main goals are:

- to break us out of our habit-bound thinking
- to produce a set of ideas from which we can choose.

Brainstorming is useful for attacking specific problems or issues where a collection of good, fresh, new ideas are needed.

Brainstorming can take place either individually or in a group of two or more. The best results are obtained when the following guidelines are observed:

1 Think freely

All ideas are written down, without judging how good they are. Children often fall into the trap of thinking only one idea or solution is needed and that every idea is either right or wrong. When we are brainstorming we shower as many thoughts as we can on a given topic. Judgement is suspended. Evaluation is reserved for later.

2 Think widely

Odd ideas and connections are fine. In fact, in every session, there may be ideas so bizarre they make the group laugh. By permitting children to think outside the boundaries of ordinary, normal thought, new ideas and solutions may arise.

3 Think more deeply

Concentrate on generating a large stock of ideas so that later on they can be sifted through. There are two reasons for wanting a large quantity. First, the obvious, usual, stale, unworkable ideas seem to come to mind first: these ideas are probably not going to be fresh or creative. Second, the larger your list of possibilities, the more you will have to choose from, adapt, or combine. Some brainstormers aim for a fixed number, like 10, 20 or 50 ideas.

Decide on a focus or problem for a brainstorming session. Ask the children to generate as many ideas as they can about a given topic. This is the thought shower. Keep the session relaxed and playful. Limit the session. A typical session should be limited to five or ten minutes. You might want them to put the list in an order or decide what they think are the best ideas and why.

Thinking processes: Brainstorming, creative thinking, evaluating

Links: Make a List, p.34; Picture This, p50; What Do You Think?, p.66

Starters for thinking

Choose one of the following topics for a brainstorming session. Generate at least as many ideas as you can. Then decide what you think are your three best ideas.

- A new snack food
- How to keep rowdy children quiet on a school bus
- How to get more tourists to visit … (your country, town, area)
- How to be healthy
- How to keep a toddler happy
- A name for a new breakfast cereal
- How to keep your keys safe
- A new toy
- A new electronic computer game
- A new machine
- Ways to decorate a cow
- New games for the Olympics
- Ideas for school trips.
- Name for a pop group
- Fundraising ideas for school

26 Visualisation

'In my head I can see forever.' Jan, age 10

Guided imagery or visualisation can be a powerful stimulus to creative thinking. It can be used as a form of meditation (see p.36) to focus the mind or stimulate creative thinking through guided images. It uses 'the inner eye' to create and explore special places in the mind. A focus such as a candle flame, picture or word stimulus can be used to practise concentrating the mind and to exercise visual thinking and imagination. For example, children might be asked to close their eyes and visualise a pool of still water, the warmth of the sun or their body filled with light. Such experiences can be remarkably effective in stilling the mind and focusing it on positive images and emotions.

Visualisation is also a way in which children can be helped to focus on their own potential and positive qualities, such as calmness, patience and goodwill, either held in the mind or directed towards other people. This can be effective in building a positive self image and inspiring a realisation of one's own goodness.

These processes of meditative practice and visualisation can develop a range of skills, including the ability to relax, to still the mind, to create visual images, to concentrate on a single focus, and to control mind and body. Guided imagery gives you, the facilitator, an opportunity to exercise and develop your own creativity, allowing your experience and intuition to guide the child's imaginary journey. You can take them on an imaginary journey in their mind's eye – into space, under the sea, or shrunk to the size of an insect. Ask what they see, feel, hear, smell and taste. You may want to play a recorded journey. Later you may wish to allow the class the chance to choose the theme of the guided journey.

The following are hints on how to facilitate guided imagery:

- explain the aims of the session
- use a visual aid, e.g. a poster
- keep sessions short
- start with a short relaxation exercise
- speak slowly, in the 'here and now'
- ask questions along the way
- pause to experience stillness
- use all the senses in your guided journey
- incorporate a happy surprise
- return back from your journey, ending in a brief silence

Guided imagery can take almost any subject as its starting point: for example, a journey down a street, a woodland walk or a flight in the air. After the journey ends give children an opportunity to talk about their journey. Discuss the difference between a real journey and a journey in the mind.

Thinking processes: Focused attention, concentration, visualisation

Links: Meditation, p.36.

Starters for thinking

- Imagine the blue sky. Empty your mind so that you can only see the blue sky. If you have a thought, visualise it as a cloud and watch it slowly move across the sky and disappear ...
- Imagine you are in your favourite place. It could be a real place like a room or an imaginary place. Imagine you are there. Notice the colours, shapes and sounds. What does it feel like to be there? What is good about being there?
- Imagine a white screen. On the screen you see the outline of a house. Now you see a door. What colour is it? Now you see each of the windows. Now you see the roof. The house is being coloured. Now you see the garden. There is a gate into the garden. You open it and go into the garden. What do you see ... ?
- Imagine you are holding the object that you are most fond of. It might be a teddy, or toy, a beautiful shell or stone, or a model you have made. Think how it feels to touch and hold it. Is it hard or soft, rough or smooth, warm or cold ... ? Look at it very carefully. Slowly turn it over. Now carefully put it back in a special place, a place where you can always find it.
- Imagine a pool of water in your mind. Imagine the pool being utterly still, without a ripple to disturb the surface. Find yourself thinking of nothing but the smooth surface of the water.
- Imagine you are on a beach. You are going to walk along the beach. Feel the sand as you walk. Listen to the sound of the sea. There is someone with you. Who is there? Look around on the beach. What do you see? What do you feel?
- Imagine a situation which makes you feel tense or angry. Tell yourself you can handle this. Picture yourself dealing with the situation calmly and strongly.
- Imagine a day that starts sunny, becomes cloudy, then stormy, then sunny again.
- Imagine a country scene which changes from spring to summer, autumn, winter and spring again.
- Look in the mirror. 'See' yourself wearing different kinds of clothes. What are they? What colour are they?
- Imagine yourself making a journey to a toyshop or pet shop. You see everything inside it. What special toy or pet will you choose?
- Visualise the person you most admire (or a flower, a circle or other shape, a peaceful place, a walk in a forest) ...

27 What Do You Think ... ?

'*I sometimes have thoughts no-one else has.*' Tarik, age 9

We all know something that no-one else knows, and this may include what we think or feel about any given topic. There are of course people who cannot resist telling us everything they do know about a topic. Equally there are others who, for one reason or another, rarely disclose or share what they know and feel.

If we want our children to have the confidence to say and share what they want to say, to have 'the gift of tongues' that is the fluency to put into words their thoughts and feelings, we need to give them opportunities to practise this. One way is to have a Learning Board, where at the end of the day children jot down what they think they learned that day.

Another way is to find a stimulus for their creative thinking. There are four aspects of creative thinking that have long been identified in research, namely:

- fluency
- flexibility
- originality
- elaboration

'What do you think about ... ?' is a strategy that challenges children to say all they can about a given topic. We want them to say what they know, but also what they think (which may include saying what they do not know) and what they feel, their emotional response and experience of this topic. Can they say something interesting about ... ? What one teacher does is to put a stimulus word or phrase on the board first thing in the morning for the children to respond to. They are then invited to share their thoughts with their partner, then with the rest of the class. With practice, children's responses tend to become more fluent and interesting.

Thinking processes: Creative thinking, me-cognition, memory

Links: About Me, p.14; Problem Solving, p.54; Questions for Thinking, p.56; Would You Rather ... ?, p.72

Starters for thinking

What do you know, think or feel about ...

- blue?
- fashion?
- sport?
- cars?
- cats (or dogs)?
- kings and queens of England?
- spiders (or any other kind of creature)?
- food?
- rainbows?
- computer games?

- What do you think about ... (a topical issue)?
- What do you think could be behind this door? (*Draw an interesting door.*)
- What do you think this saying means? 'You have to be put in prison to be set free.'
- If you had a crystal ball and could see the future in it, what do you think you would see?
- What is your favourite invention? Give five or more reasons why.
- What is the best season of the year – spring, summer, autumn or winter? Why? Give five or more reasons for your choice.
- Are boys and girls treated differently? Should they be?
- The ancient Greeks thought of seven wonders in their world. What would be the seven wonders in *your* world be (people, places, activities, feelings, smells)?
- Is it better to be a child or adult? Why?

28 What If ... ?

'*What if you were the only person left in the world?*' Kirsten, age 10

The basis of creative or hypothetical thinking is the question 'What if ... ?' Every 'What if ... ' question creates a new but possible world, and invites children to consider what the consequences of that hypothesis might be. 'What if ... ?' starters are not simply exercises in make-believe. They invite children to extend their thinking by considering the consequences of an imagined situation. 'What if ... ?' can be used to develop the four aspects of creative thinking:

- fluency of ideas – how many 'What ifs' can you think of?
- flexibility of ideas – what different 'What ifs' can you think of?
- originality of ideas – what 'What if?' is there that nobody has thought of?
- elaboration of ideas – what are the possible consequences of a 'What if?'

'What ifs?' provide possible starting points for discussion and writing, or for a follow-up speaking and listening game. For example, after children have had a chance to think, ask them to write and share ideas. Can they talk for one minute (or half a minute) without a break on the given 'What if?' question?

'What ifs' can provide a wishful-thinking kind of challenge by adding some impossible feature, or by picking out some part of an item and imagining it was missing. For example what essential features of the following could you imagine leaving out of a house, school, bicycle, library, birthday? (e.g. 'What if your house had no ... ?'). What features could you imagine adding to school, parents, clothes, sleep, sports? (e.g. 'Wouldn't it be nice if...')

Can you or your children create ten 'What if ...' impossibilities? Choose, draw and discuss your most interesting idea. Ask them, for example:

- *Can you make up your own 'What if?' question?*
- *How many 'What if?' questions can you make up?*
- *Which is the most interesting 'What if?' question?*
- *Can you think of a 'What if?' question that could never come about? Why?*

Ask children to select from a list what they think is the most interesting or creative question and to say why. Which question(s) have they never thought about before?

Discuss whether it is helpful to think about 'What if ...' questions (hypotheses). When is it useful to think of the consequences of what might happen? Why? Is it better to think of many possibilities or to have one idea? Why? What helps you to have a good ideas?

Thinking processes: Evaluating, hypothesising, questioning, reasoning

Links: Philosophical Questions, p.48; What Do You Think?, p.66; Would You Rather ... ?, p.72

Starters for thinking

- What if animals could speak?
- What if you had eyes in the back of your head?
- What if you were turned into a frog?
- What if you could travel in time? Where would you go? Why?
- What if you could become invisible? When would you want to? Why?
- What if no-one had a nose?
- What if a toy could come to life? Which toy would you want it to be? Why?
- What if people could fly?
- What if no-one could speak?
- What if plants started to walk?
- What if no-one needed to go to sleep?
- What if people discovered the secret of eternal life?
- What if the oceans all dried up?
- What if there were another Ice Age?
- What if you won a prize of £1000?
- What if you were given your own TV station to run?
- What if there were no teachers in school?
- What if you could repeat a favourite moment in your life? Which would it be?
- What if you had a magic carpet? Where would you choose to go? Why?
- What if you were a superhero, what powers would you want to have and why?
- What if you had another eye? Where would you put it and why?
- What if you could only see black and white? What could you do/ not do?
- What if you were locked in an empty room for an hour, how would you pass the time? What else might you do?
- If only ...

29 Word Play

'*Where do words come from?*' Carl, age 6

Words are the tools for creative thinking, and what more typical way for children to be creative than through humour. Humans are the only animals that laugh. Jokes can be seen as a form of creative thinking, testing and expanding a child's imagination, guessing powers, and memory. Jokes create vivid pictorial images that can fire a child's imagination. Riddles, either joke-riddles or true riddles, stimulate divergent thinking and critical response. Riddles highlight the contrast between appearance and reality, between that which has to be guessed and that which appears at first sight. They stimulate by being enigmatic and puzzling.

A popular word game is 'How many words can you make from ... (any given word or set of letters)?' A variation of this is to award points for words of different lengths, e.g. 1 point for three-letter words, 2 for four-letter words, 5 for five-letter words and so on – or a point for every letter used in a word.

There are plenty of opportunities for challenging word play with children by adapting popular commercial games. Boggle is a popular word game, using nine letters in a grid, easily reproduced in the classroom. For example: how many words can you make using these letters:

E	L	S
R	A	I
T	O	P

Another popular game is scrabble. Display some sets of scrabble letters and see what words (and scores) children can make with them. For example:

Anagrams are another popular type of word puzzle. What words are GANRE and TARIL anagrams of? Every five-letter anagram has 120 possible letter arrangements so there is much scope here for practising trial-and-error strategies. There may of course be more than one answer, for example GANRE = range and anger, TARIL = trail and trial. Extend the puzzle to more of an open-ended investigation by seeing what 3,4,5 letter anagrams children can invent. Can they find anagrams with more than one answer?

Thinking processes: Creative thinking, classifying, information processing, reasoning

Links: Alphabeticals, p.16; Make a List, p.34

Starters for thinking

- How many words can you think of to use instead of 'said' to describe how people say things, e.g. shout, whisper, mumble etc.?
- Think of twenty words beginning with 'S' (or any other letter). Sort them into different groups.
- How many different words can you make from the letters of the word 'rumplestiltskin'? (Or 'chrysanthemum' or any other long word)
- Invent five new words and say what they mean.
- How many words can you think of which mean 'moving' in some way e.g. hop, leap, limp, crawl, etc.?
- How many words can you think of that rhyme with … (e.g. 'play', 'fish', 'moon', 'white', 'cat', 'feet')? Write a poem using some of these rhyming words.
- Invent a code using numbers for letters. Write a secret message to someone.
- Create a story which contains these words … (e.g. 'When he woke up the dinosaur was still there.')
- Think of five clues to make up a riddle about an object or person.
- Make up a tongue twister which includes your name (or the name of a friend).
- Make up a word chain where the letters at the end of each word must also begin the next word e.g. shop, hope, open.
- What other words could be used instead of 'nice' (or 'good')?
- Create a wordsearch using words connected to … (e.g. food).
- Describe an orange in ten different ways. (*Give each child an orange to study.*)
- Use the initials of your name to write an acrostic poem about yourself (or somebody else, an animal, a season etc.).
- (*Show two or more words, sentences, pictures, objects.*) Link these two in as interesting a way as possible in a short story.
- Choose sets of two or three letters, e.g. HT, TPS, UFO. What might the letters stand for? What might they be an acronym for? (e.g. HT = Hot Teacher, High Tide, Hairy Toes etc.)
- Anagrams. This jumbled word is a part of the body: *adeh* (head). Create anagrams for other parts of the body. Try them on your partner.

30 Would You Rather ... ?

'*Why is life so full of difficult choices?*' Sophie, age 9

A simple way to challenge children's thinking is to offer them two things and ask them to make a choice between them by asking 'Which would you prefer?' or 'Would you rather ... ?' The choice might for example be between two objects, pictures, texts, persons, places, feelings, states, activities, words or imaginary things. A simple choice between one or the other might be easy; the follow-up adds challenge – 'Say *why*.' And a further challenge can be added by saying ' ... and give as many reasons as possible.'

The picture book *Would You Rather?* by John Burningham presents a range of imaginary dilemmas. Each page illustrates a choice, for example: Would you rather live in a house surrounded by the sea, by snow or by jungle? After reading the book *Would You Rather?*, ask children to think up different sorts of dilemmas themselves. Examples from children have included: Would you rather be a horse, a dog, a pig or a spider? Would you rather be a giant or a dwarf? Would you rather have a million pounds and be rich, or be poor and live forever?

When asked whether she would rather be a bird or a butterfly, and to give as many reasons as possible for her choice, a girl responded: 'I would like to be a butterfly. I would like to be a peacock butterfly because I like their pretty colours and you can go on holiday without paying and ... ' and added a list of seven more reasons. When asked: 'Would you rather be old or young?' a boy responded 'Young, because when you are young you have more chance of getting older ... '

The following are some starters for thinking involving choices and reasons for choices.

Thinking processes: Decision making, imagination, reasoning

Links: About Me, p.14; Problem Solving, p.54; Questions for Thinking, p.56; What If?, p.68

Starters for thinking

Choose which you would rather be. Give as many reasons as you can for your choice. Would you rather be ...

- a bird or a butterfly?
- a child or an adult?
- rich or happy?
- a boy or a girl?
- yourself, or someone else?
- a cat or a mouse?
- red or green?
- yes or no?
- a forest or a stream?
- rich or happy?
- a table or a chair?

- Would you rather live in the country or the town?
- Would you rather be a brick or a feather?
- Would you rather be a tree or a flower?
- Would you rather have £50 or five friends? Say why.
- Would you rather live in this country or another country? Say why.
- Would you rather live at this time or at another time in history? Say why.
- Would you rather have one good friend or £1000? Say why.
- Would you rather go through a door to another world or have free sweets for the rest of your life? Why?
- Would you rather be a colour or a sound? Which colour or sound? Why?
- Which would you rather be, a door, a window or a hole in the roof? Why?
- Would you rather live in a house surrounded by the sea, or by snow, or by the jungle? Why?

Appendix

Can you get through the mazes?

Draw your own maze.

This is a tangram. What shapes can you see? Make your own 7 piece tangram. What designs can you make from these pieces for others to create?

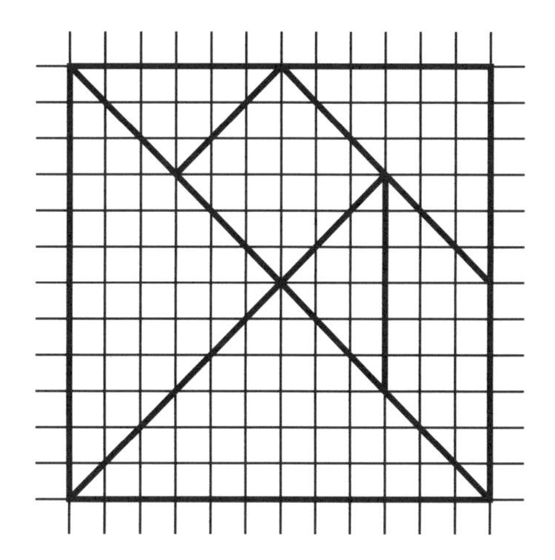

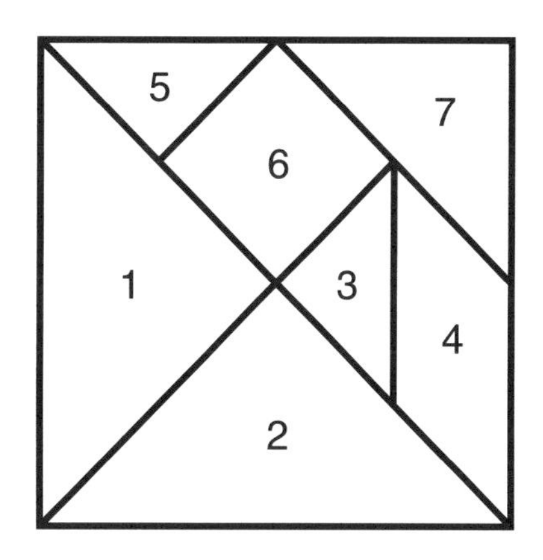

For more on Creative Shapes, see p.21.